Welcome to the End of the World

Welcome to the End of the World

Prophecy, Rage, and the New Age

Teresa Kennedy

M. Evans and Company, Inc.
New York

M. Evans and Company, Inc.
216 East 49th Street
New York, New York 10017

Library of Congress Cataloging-in-Publication Data
Kennedy, Teresa.
Welcome to the end of the world : prophecy, rage, and the New Age /
Teresa Kennedy.
p. cm.
ISBN 0-87131-817-2
1. Prophecies (Occultism)—United States. 2. End of the world—
Miscellanea. 3. Millennialism—United States. 4. New Age movement—
United States. 5. Twenty-first century—Forecasts. 6. United States—
Religion—1960– I. Title.
BF1812.U6K46 1997   133.3—DC21   96-53032
CIP

Design and type formatting by Bernard Schleifer.

Manufactured in the United States of America

9 8 7 6 5 4 3 2 1

For my daughter Zoe,
whose name means both life and joy,
and who makes thinking about the
future very important, indeed.
And for all the children of the present
age, who will live the things we can
only speculate about. May you live in
the best of times.

Acknowledgments

Special thanks to Jessica Wolf for her tireless research, help, and patience as the concept and direction of this book evolved. Without her help there would be no book—thank you. Special thanks to Chris Rutkowski for permission to reprint "A Unified Theory of Alien Incompetence," and for reminding us that humor will thankfully have a place in the world to come.

Contents

Welcome to the End of the World

Introduction
WHAT ARE WE
WAITING FOR?

THINK ABOUT IT. Has your otherwise ordinary spouse suddenly converted to the channeled teachings of a nonincarnate entity from Alpha Centauri? Has your secretary become a born-again Buddhist? Perhaps a friend or relative has recently confided a heretofore unsuspected history of alien-abduction memories? Did your longtime drinking buddy give up the pleasures of beer and pinball for herbal fasts and yogic meditation? Has the executive type down the street absconded with company funds to live the life of a hardcore survivalist on the top of some mountain in Idaho? Or perhaps even you yourself are furtively packing crystals and chamomile tea in lieu of Excedrin and Maalox to help you cope?

This book attempts to address a relatively simple question:

What the heck is going on?

No one, it seems, is safe from the coming New Age. As the year 2000 approaches, society finds itself in the throes of that nebulous thing called "change."

1

Predictions and forecasters crop up on every street-corner. The bookstores overflow with a plethora of "guides" for the millennium. Followers of New Age "prophets" have been known to garner Federal monies for "training programs" that are subsequently exposed as "cults" of psychological abuse.

And still, we are delirious with the possibilities of far-reaching, sometimes catastrophic and sometimes utopian concepts of the world to come. Whether the vision of tomorrow is secular or spiritual, whether the forecaster is an economist, a politician, mystic, or a scholarly iconoclast—if they seem to have an idea of what to expect as the century turns—we're ready to listen.

We want change, need change—demand it of ourselves, of our loved ones, and of society as a whole. As we face the coming turn of the century, we perceive the past as imperfect, the future as uncertain. As the saying goes, something's got to give. And if the dis-ease we feel might be called millennial fever, then its principal symptom is surely the expectation of far-reaching and widespread transformation of the world as we understand it. Politicians get elected on platforms of "change," while soothsayers, futurists, and cognoscenti from all walks of life attain overnight celebrity by assuring us that the "change" is coming. The nature of this transformation varies with the commentator. We are variously promised earth changes, spiritual changes, economic changes, political changes, societal changes, and changes from within. One thing all of the prophecies and predictions do hold dear, however, is that the promised changes will be big. Real big. If change is good, the theory would indicate that apocalypse—total transformation—is even better.

But for all our love of change, it seems that no one has a very clear notion of just what exactly it is that we're changing into. And—even in the midst of the great millennial soup bubbling all around us— that, at least, seems to remain a matter of opinion. On one side, a host of publications, broadcasts, and books spill forth from the media machine to assure us that our human history of aggression, transgression, and unredeemed wholesale plunder has brought us teetering on the brink of personal and collective annihi- lation and extinction. Whole ways of life are threatened, they tell us, and will fall by the wayside if something is not done. A recent sampling of books and articles indicates that we are witnessing "The End" of a host of things—education, economics, and the rain forests, to name only a few. Whenever and wherever The End comes, it's selling like hotcakes. And the doomsayers abound.

In contradiction, more beneficent futurists have rushed forward to comfort us with the equally dubious notion that the terrors of these coming apocalyptic changes are only a messy and inconvenient sort of prelude to a brave new universe—a whole new consciousness; a better, newer world than the one that came before. Judging from the popular literature on the subject, the coming world is one that will be presumably populated only by the spiritually enlight- ened, the organically grown, and the cellulite-free. Not to mention the alien/human hybrids, angels, and "star people" from all over the universe. All we must do to join these Chosen, it seems, is to be adequately "prepared."

The concept of preparedness has in turn given rise to a whole industry dedicated to personal enlightenment and self-improvement. We go in search of wholeness and wellness like pilgrims on the road to the Holy Land. We practice "safe" sex and sobriety. We are drug-free, fat-free, and smoke-free. We are obsessed with exercise and eating right; all trying to climb on the bandwagon of a newly secularized spirituality, attempting to stave off mortality with magical thinking.

Welcome to the End of the World attempts to examine the phenomena of millennialism in popular culture by concentrating on the three key areas of Prophecy, Rage, and the so-called New Age. Part I examines the prophets of the past, famous prophecies considered in historical context, and finally, the "prophetic" personality. As such, it addresses the spectacularly nonspecific content of some popular prophecy as well as prophecy's tendency to be self-fulfilling or, at the very least, self-adjusting in terms of interpretation. In addition, we will look at the prophetic personality in psychological terms—what is it exactly that turns someone into a divinely inspired visionary? And why do the visions always end in images of destruction? Just as prophecy itself has some important recurring motifs, an examination of the lives of many "divinely inspired" prophets yields some important biographical similarities. What those similarities add up to in the end could turn out to be the most important message of all. All the divine window-dressing aside, prophecies and the people who make them are an important metaphor for the process of the kind of personal and societal reintegration that makes for growth. Prophecy, with its rich storehouse of symbolic language and mysterious allegory, serves to remind us of who we are and where we came from.

It enables alienated people to join in systems of shared belief. And for that reason alone it is valuable.

As the personality goes, so goes society. And, in fact, during millennial periods in history, society as a whole begins to exhibit the same symptoms of paranoid disorder as exist in individuals. Part II traces the origins of this collective paranoia through feelings of rage and loss of control. As a society we are fearful because we know we have been lied to—because we have passed important points in our collective history without changing anything at all. We have been promised a great deal but have realized little in the way of gain and fulfillment. Rage develops because on a fundamental level we know that we do not exercise the degree of control over our lives and destinies that we are "supposed" to. Crime increases, economies crumble, and life becomes more and more uncertain. Seemingly "stuck" in our lives, we begin to project—to suspect that the change we crave will come necessarily from some unstoppable outside force—god, nuclear war, the intervention of hostile extraterrestrial intelligence, the earth tilting upon its axis, etc.

Faced, then, with the enormity of forces truly beyond individual control and with the possibility of destruction those forces traditionally contain, we begin to look to the possibility of redemption—of somehow being spared from destruction. And we begin to seek our salvation through the forces of spiritual life—to find a means of becoming one of the Chosen.

Part III, "The New Age," examines some of the spiritual and quasi-spiritual movements of both current and past periods in history. In seeking spirituality through various forms of religion and otherwise magical systems of thought, we are trying perhaps to

redeem and prepare ourselves for the terrors of apocalyptic change, but we are also reasserting our sense
of control over our lives and environments. Afflicted
as we are by collective paranoia, we manifest increased
spirituality either in purification movements (self-
improvement and wellness), in otherworldliness
(angels, aliens, and other "rescuers"), or by embracing
the magical-thought systems of "lost" cultures and
indigenous religions—believing perhaps that the
answer lies not in looking to the future, but somewhere
in the past.

Finally, it is not the intention of this book to
disparage millennialism in any of its aspects—only
to examine it in human, rather than historic, terms.
Nor is it my wish to purport my own theories of what
the future may hold—either in disastrous or utopian
visions of what may come. Rather, I want only to
remind the reader that as human beings we have the
capacity to create either future—and that we always
hold the power to create the change we so desperately
seek, both as individuals and as a society. For this
reason I tend to focus on the "spiritual" atmosphere
that surrounds the coming millennium, rather
than to address the fashions in more secular types of
future casting.

And for all the identifiable psychology surrounding the approach of the millennium, it is my
opinion that psychology and what we have come to call
spirituality are not so easily separated. Whatever your
personal predictions for the year 2000, the answers are
perhaps not as important as the questions. And our
thoughts about the future seem to come down to the
eternal questions: Did we create god or did god create
us? Will our world end at our own hand, or will it end

at god's? Is the future itself still a matter of our own choosing, and can it yet be shaped by spiritual forces such as faith and goodness and love?

No matter what side of those debates you come out on, our struggles with the future would appear to offer some valuable clues:

1. The fact that we share the capacity to respond to the symbolic and ancient language of spirituality could eventually provide a basis for a kind of global unification that has heretofore been ignored in the search for individual and collective identity, and

2. That the symbolic messages and motifs of prophecy may contain a kind of collective description not of the future of the world, but of the journey of man. By pondering the mysteries put forth in areas like prophecy and spiritual tradition, we are, in effect, reintegrating and reempowering important aspects of human nature both collectively and individually. We are reminding ourselves of who we are, and giving ourselves the power to shape our future.

For this reason, I am content to consider the future as essentially unpredictable, though in many aspects, human beings are very predictable. From the moment that humankind began to be aware of time, we have attempted to imbue time with meaning by marking its passage. Every season, every birthday, every New Year's Eve constitutes an occasion to pause to take stock of what has gone before, to think and to dream about what will come. Faced with the marker of a thousand years, we are faced with the opportunity to broaden our perspective on the past and the future in a way that will not come again in any of our lifetimes. And whether you greet the year 2000 filled with hope or filled with anxiety, filled with rage or filled with promise, I would only ask that you allow that these occasions by which we mark the passing of the ages are also marked by our unique human ability to take stock of ourselves and our world. And that it is perhaps this ability alone that makes our progress possible. The changes that can be realized in moments like this, however small or subtle they may seem, can add up over time to the realization of a larger dream.

PART I
PROPHECY

One

A CRASH COURSE IN THE DIVINE

THE *RANDOM HOUSE DICTIONARY* defines the word "prophecy" as

> 1) the foretelling or prediction of what is to come;
> 2) something that is declared by a prophet, esp. a divinely inspired prediction, instruction or exhortation;
> 3) a divinely inspired utterance or revelation.

A "prophet," on the other hand, is defined as "a person who speaks for God, or a deity, or by divine inspiration." The definition goes on to include a number of subcategories of prophets as defined by the Old Testament, and further defines these elusive creatures as "a person regarded as, or claiming to be, an inspired leader or teacher," or a "spokesperson for some doctrine, cause or movement."

In short, it appears to be far easier to come up with a definition for prophecy than it is to define a prophet. Prophecy seems to require the element of divine inspiration; prophets, on the other hand, have only to make the claim that they are prophets in order to become prophets. Still, if religion is "the opiate of the people," prophecy is certainly the addiction of the millennialist. The future has become its own kind of high, one that takes us out of a messy and unmanageable present reality and into the world of possibility.

Since we generally associate the power of prophecy with knowing the future, the relative truth of the prophet's message resides not so much in objective proof—which only time can provide—but more or less in the eyes and ears of the beholder. We can choose to believe that a given prediction will happen or choose not to believe it. But this is the very kind of choice that shapes our actions, our philosophy, and our future.

With the millennium looming on the collective horizon, it seems only right that the prophecy business is booming. From the Virgin Mary and Nostradamus to the channeled messages of New Age gods like Ramtha and Michael, we find ourselves with a truly bewildering array of prophets and prophecies, past and present, to choose from in our search for an answer to that perennial question—what does the future hold?

The ancient Israelites had a sure test for the authenticity of a prophet's message—if a prophecy didn't come true, the prophet was simply killed. And while it remains to be seen whether it is to our credit that we have ceased to shoot the messenger, modern times provide for a greater degree of leniency in dealing with such visionaries, and so opens the door for considerable latitude for interpretation of what they have to say.

Boiled down to its essentials, though, prophetic tradition appears to revolve around a single, oft-repeated refrain: "You must be very, very good or something very, very bad will surely happen." But then again, the simplicity of that message doesn't necessarily make it any less profound. And there are certainly a number of interesting variations on the theme, i.e., "If only a few of you are very, very good, maybe there's still a chance." "If a few of you become heartfelt vegetarians and move to the Northwest and work to stop animal testing, maybe the rest will fall into the ocean but you might have a fighting chance." And, finally, "Pray people. Pray unceasingly. Ponder the mystery, look within and try to get it through your thick, barbarian skulls that it's up to you."

It's important to remember that prophecies are frequently presented in symbolic, rather than specific, language. Divinatory practices as the Tarot, Western and Eastern astrology, and oracles, such as rune stones or the I Ching, are all methods that human beings have used since ancient times to try to access a future vision—and each of those methods uses a symbolic language to communicate. And perhaps those symbolic systems are useful as a means of bypassing the rationalist or the cynic in all of us because they cause us to think differently about reality, and to respond emotionally, rather than rationally, to the message. Without things like emotion involved, it can be all too easy to reject ephemera such as the notion that if you are good, life will get better as just too simple.

The problem with prophetic prediction begins when people start to insist that symbolism is science. It is not. Prophecy is not so much a vision of what will be, as it is a map of what might be. A prophecy putting forth exact dates and times is relatively rare and any specificity is frequently imposed on the original message through a variety of interpreters, reinterpreters, and apologists. Which is not to mention that any prophecy is also necessarily filtered through the individual ego and personality of the prophet, factors that are more than capable of coloring any "divine" inspiration.

It may very well be possible for some people to dip in and out of the river of time, see the future, and clarify or warn us about impending events. I'm not about to say they can't. But at the risk of de-mystifying a cherished tradition, I will say that *how* we are transformed or inspired by prophetic information will depend on who we are in the first place, what degree of specificity or "science" we feel compelled to impose on symbolic and allegorical language, and what we already believe is possible.

As we approach the turn of the century, we are increasingly obsessed with what the future holds. The reasons for this are quite varied, yet all are universally human. They range from a need to give the passing of years new meaning— just as we do on New Year's Eve or on a birthday—to a sense that the world is faced with an unprecedented radical degeneration of civilization as we understand it. There are some who view the millennium as a kind of ultimate opportunity to embrace spiritual and personal transformation. There are those who think the world is going to hell and those who believe that it already has. Still others hold to the interesting idea that we are nervous about what is to come because we are already living the future—a future that, according to the prophets, was never supposed to happen. We are nervous because we have survived the predictions thus far. We dropped the atom bomb, we walked on the moon, ended the Cold War and saw the dissolution of Apartheid in South Africa. Where is there left to go? If this time is borrowed time, who is to be paid back?

It is a mistake to generalize the reasons for wanting to know the future. They are as individual as people are. Yet, if we have different reasons for looking toward the future, whatever meaning we find in prophecy and prediction comes out of our past—the affirmation of ideas, symbols, and concepts that are firmly rooted in inner consciousness, in our mythology, and in our collective memory. Whatever particular brand of prophecy you prefer, you can count on its being presented in recognizable terms—using a symbolic vocabulary guaranteed to push the necessary psychospiritual buttons.

Too often, however, we hear prophetic forecasts and future predictions without the faintest notion of where they come from, much less give any thought to why we respond the way we do. And in evaluating a forecast or prediction, it's important to have some context—if only for purposes of self-recognition.

Author Peter Stearns, in his book *Millennium III Century XXI* has identified four steps in identifying and evaluating forecasts. Though Stearns's work concentrates on the secular arena, his ideas do have a great deal of merit when applied to the mystical or "divinely inspired." For purposes of this discussion, my use of the term "divinely inspired" includes any prophecy or prediction that is reported to come from a source that might be considered "otherworldly," including god and his minions, channeled "spiritual" presences, aliens, and what have you.

First, Stearns says we must remember that any prophecy or prediction is essentially a guess, and that guesses are very often wrong. Second, we should determine whether the nature of a prediction is optimistic or pessimistic or neutral. Third, Stearns insists that we must identify those predictions that seem to be merely a kind of extrapolation and projection of things that are currently going on. And, fourth, we must identify the range of the prediction. Is it mindlessly deterministic? Does it depend on one set of factors to shape the future? On what assumptions is the prediction based?

Clearly, these four criteria could (and perhaps should) be applied to the host of "mystical" or "divinely inspired" predictions and prophecies that are crowding the current marketplace as human society marches toward the millennium. Yet it is not really in human nature to scrutinize the divine too closely, and likewise, mystical messages, by and large, are not subject to much examination. Perhaps because our collective need to believe is far more powerful than our need to be rational, cynical, or even entirely sane.

The human response to the mystical is an emotional, non-rational response. It is a function of the subconscious mind, and the impulse to make subconscious knowledge conscious reality is universal. If we believe that we are on the threshold of a whole New Age, we have new hope. And hope is perhaps more important to the future than the more rational or realistic contention that things will plod along pretty much as they have done for the next thousand years.

The impulse to integrate the mystical, mythological, and spiritual realms with the rational and "real" is important if only because it is an impulse to integrate. Viewed from a strictly psychological standpoint, integration and the resulting wholeness is what makes growth possible. And if that can be said to be true in the context of individual personality, it is also true for society.

The impulse itself can arise from dissatisfaction or need, awareness of social movements, or individual personality. It is not so much determined by a date on a calendar or the year 2000 as it is by the fact that a calendar or a date has become a symbol of how we humans give time meaning. Big dates, therefore, lend themselves to the search for big meanings. For most people, the passing of a fortieth birthday is "bigger" than a thirtieth, a fiftieth birthday is "bigger" still. The passing of a century, then, would seem to be positively fraught with meaning. And the passing of a millennium is quite literally awe-inspiring.

And if we look for awe or inspiration we can find it in prophecy. Enough at least to adequately nourish the sense of a larger reality than the one in which we are forced to spend our days. Divinely inspired messages and prophecies form a rich part of our historical, philosophical, and religious traditions; and belief in prophecy links us to a powerful collective tradition. Through belief, we become part of the human community. The origins and messages of prophecy are mysterious to us, yet its themes are relevant and applicable to our lives. We are awed—we become part of a larger plan. We find meaning in those mysteries, not by subjecting them to rational criteria, but by pondering the nature of mystery itself. And perhaps that is ultimately to our credit. We are able to imbue our lives with newness and promise simply by reminding ourselves, from time to time, that we don't know everything. We respond to and believe in mysteries on a fundamental level, and by doing that we reintegrate and become a little more divine that we were before. And we are able, through simple belief in the simple truths of prophecy, to revitalize our own existence. As only a glance at the world around you will tell you, that quality can make for a wealth of delusion, but it can also make for miracles.

Two

PROPHECY'S GREATEST HITS

Three Visions

WE FACE THE TURN of the coming millennium with a range of possibilities already in place, both collectively and individually. On the one side we have the doomsday scenario. The possibilities here include the biblical story of Apocalypse, a reckoning of souls in a final Judgment and the coming or second coming of a Messiah. More secularized versions of doomsday include visions of unheard-of natural disasters, global destruction through war, and an assortment of other retributions. Generally speaking, in the doomsday scenario, life on earth, or "time" as we know it, ends as a result of our "sins"—whether they take the form of sins against god, against the earth, or against each other.

On the more upbeat side, we can find more utopian, heavenly or New Age visions of the future, including a turning away from technology and back to the land; the exaltation of "lost" skills such as artisanship; and the formation of small self-sufficient communities of people with similar philosophies. In addition, there are those who further gild the New Age lily with assurances of global peace, and world-wide political or spiritual enlightenment, The Age of Aquarius, interstellar communications with beings from other planets, and so forth.

A third (and by far the most popular) idea of life in the coming century seems to combine pessimistic and optimistic visions: The construct of a progressive and enlightened, phoenix-like civilization formed on the ashes of the old world—a renewal in the life of man, predicated by some necessary destruction and purification.

Each of these mystical visions of the world to come is important because each speaks to an essential aspect of the human character and condition. No matter what your individual prophetic preference, we have only to look around to observe that each of these visions of the future is already in active rehearsal in the present, just as each has, to some extent, been drawn from the experiences of the past.

But what do these seemingly contradictory ideas of the future really mean? How is all this "symbolic language" to be interpreted in human terms?

Visions of doomsday arise out of fear and fear gives rise to the need to survive. Proponents of a coming Armageddon, whether biblically inspired or not, are, in embracing that vision, seeking ways to survive a coming destruction in both physical and spiritual terms. Hence we can trace the rise of survivalist

movements of all kinds—militias, religious funda-
mentalists, the rage for "physical fitness" and "back
to basics."

The survivalist vision is certainly informed by
biblical literature, but in a larger sense, it can be seen
as a sense of crisis expressed in authoritarian terms.
In many ways, survivalist movements represent more
than just the need for personal survival, or a struggle
against mortality. Though admittedly the certainty
of death is easier to face when death takes place on
a planetary scale rather than on an individual one,
survivalists also represent a storehouse of traditional
values, morals, and ways of thinking about the world.
The survivalist vision is essentially a warrior's stance.
And, in taking that stance, participants in movements of this kind are preparing themselves to fight
the decline of values, to participate in the struggle of
good against evil, and to preserve a portion of human
history in a future world.

In contrast, the utopian vision of the future is
comprised of what might be called a naive enthusiasm.
These are the factions of society who are seeking to "go
where no one has gone before." As author Martin
Green, in his book *Prophets of a New Age* states:
"People of this type (and we are all of this type part
of the time) have a different sense of limits, and try
things [the] others wouldn't dare. They affirm
absolutes and realize ideals." The naive aspect of this
vision is characterized both by its neo-paganism
("natural" highs, herbal "cures," nature worship, etc.)
and by its return to naive or even childish values and
visions.

In the naive view, the solution to the confusion or uncertainty is to simplify; through simplicity will come transformation. In the later years of the twentieth century we have a spate of books with titles like *The Children's Book of Virtues* or *Everything I Need to Know I Learned in Kindergarten.*

This construct, by the way, is hardly a new idea. Tolstoy, a chief advocate for the wave of "New Age" thought that emerged around the turn of the last century, insisted that he had been taught all crucial values as a child, and his subsequent education had merely served to obscure them.

Today, we embrace the cult of the inner child, search for truth in naive cultures, and "return" in droves to an almost evangelical concept of humanity's essential "goodness." And, like the children they so admire, the naive group enthusiastically expects enlightenment and even salvation to come forth from "parental" or quasi-parental figures.

Interventions by advanced aliens, interbreeding with other interstellar species (a new twist on the naiveté of sexual revolution, by the way), the theory of an angelic presence on earth—all are hallmarks of the naive view. All involve an assortment of "spiritual" communication with beings from beyond, who will—when we are "ready"—place in our hands the keys to salvation.

Yet, however romantic all such visions can seem, it is the naive type who can be said to represent the cultural repository for hope. It is in the naive vision that we find not so much the exaltation of identity and ego, but the concept that "only a handful" of good people can indeed save the world.

The third type of visionary distills the fear of the future and the hope for the future into a comprehensible system or chronological progression. This group knows that fear is justified, but hope is not out of place. The third group is aware of the problems that beset the world and see them solved and progress attained through a kind of religion of sacrifice. We will be punished for our sins of excess before we can be rewarded for our love of goodness. Purification must take place before enlightenment.

Though it's important to stress that each of us can be said to belong to each of these groups at different times, the third group's hybrid approach to the millennium most clearly expresses just how blurred the boundaries can get. Survival is paramount to be sure. But survival is best attained through personal preparedness, purification, and, above all, sacrifice. We give up sugar, fat, and backyard barbecues; we exercise and eat right. We are drug-free. We give up the materialistic "fast track" to spend more time with the children. We assign an element of "realism" to the most trivial phenomena or social trend because, to the third group, crisis has become its own explanation. We lose excess emotional and psychological baggage in preparation for the new world. We willingly give up old metaphors and values; we purify and simplify our minds and bodies and we wait for what we hope will be the next revelatory step.

Finally, the third group embraces the concept of controlling their sense of crisis through organized social effort. Lobbyists, environmental movements, political watchdogs, and special-interest vigilantes all can be seen to represent this mindset. It is not enough that an individual gives up smoking cigarettes, for example; the entire planet must give up cigarettes. Such efforts are preparatory in the manner of the survivalist, but they are also naive in their enthusiasm for sacrifice. Still, because the third group embraces organized social effort, they are perhaps the most capable of shaping the future and changing the world.

In our uncertainty about the future we turn to a number of key figures whose body of prophetic work or philosophy seems to validate these three existing versions of the future. Regardless of the fact that a universal precept of both religious and spiritual law is to recognize and embrace the element of divinity that dwells within each of us—most people are far more convinced of the human capacity for divinity in man when it happens to somebody else. Rather than cultivate our own "inner voice" and heed its messages, the current vogue in prophets and prophecy can be seen as an externalization of human knowledge that cannot be "known" or gained through ordinary, rational means. Yet as part of the collective language of symbols these messages have always been with us. We consult trance mediums and spiritualists who have enlightened "entities" and "guides" who speak through them, about those things of which we are, on some level, already aware. And yet we think of these practitioners as "psychic" or otherwise "chosen." Regardless of the relative merits of the prophetic messages themselves, we never seem to question that those messages come from some source or entity apart from the individual doing the talking. As a species, we used to require that such information came from god. We have not yet come to a point, however, where we can accept the great spiritual truth that god dwells within. Perhaps we profess to know it or even to practice it, but the kind of symbolic knowledge available to us through ancient and contemporary "seers" we remain unable to accept as part of our human heritage and as part of our legacy to the future world.

The point is that most of us, no matter what our personal notions of the future, are more comfortable affirming the prophetic "powers" of a long-dead fifteenth-century courtier or some disincarnate being from Alpha Centauri than we are owning our capacity for enlightenment—our own power to draw upon inner knowledge—to predict and therefore to shape our future. And, from that, it is perhaps not too much of a leap to say that our current preoccupation with the future is not so much a matter of finding the answers as it is of our collective need to ask the questions—to reidentify—not with the predictable, but with the mysterious.

The future becomes important when the present has ceased to be satisfying. In attempting through prophecy to pin down the nature, timing, and specifics of future events, we are attempting to redefine our individual and collective roles in the chaos and uncertainty of the present. We are seeking to transform ourselves through a vision of a transformed future world. We are lost and asking for direction. There is nothing wrong with that, save our tendency to hear what we want to hear and believe what we want to believe about the road ahead and the turns that we want to make. But if the present is unsatisfying, increasingly uncertain, and chaotic, it helps to look at some of the elements that comprise that chaos.

There is almost no one, for example, who remains unaware of the global problems that threaten the modern world. Overpopulation, deforestation, pollution, civil and political unrest, all help to shape our vision of an unsatisfactory world and, not coincidentally, to shape also the predictions and prophecies that sprout up to address these problems in the context of a future society. On the more personal side, we struggle with issues of right and wrong, good and evil—relationships and responsibility—which of our brothers to "keep," and which to relinquish to their own iniquities. And in answer to our questions a host of "prophets" have arisen to help us address these issues.

Therefore, much of the prophecy and revelation arising around the turn of the present century is not so much startling for its revelatory information as it is startling in its sheer predictability. Whether apocalyptic, purified, or naively hopeful, much of the current fashion in revelation consists of visions of the future that are painted entirely in the colors of the present. The world of the future, as expressed in prophecy, comes across as a more extreme or dramatized version of the now—whatever you may believe present reality to be.

We shape the nature of prophecy by the questions and the phrasing of the questions we ask. I suspect these questions are predetermined by our collective language of symbols and mythology. The fact that we are at a time in history where we are filled with questions is all-important. No one consults an oracle or seeks out a prophet without first having a question. And no oracle, whether from this world or another, presents "answers" for questions that have yet to be asked.

If an individual believes, for example, that man's presence upon the earth is a direct threat to the earth through pollution and overpopulation, then that individual has a question or questions about that issue. He or she will doubtless respond to the "truth" of prophetic messages pointing either to positive solutions of those problems, or, more pessimistically, to the end of the problem through destruction of the populations and polluters who caused the mess in the first place.

If you are aware of the planet earth as a place with a history of destructive environmental events such as earthquakes, fires, floods and famines, you will respond to prophecies of those things happening in the future—because they are part of your present and part of your past. Part, if you will, of the collective vocabulary of destruction. For most of us, it is much easier to believe in a prediction that says the world will undergo great changes, that some will be saved and some will be destroyed by earthquakes, wars, fires, floods, and famines than it is to believe that on the last day of 1999, God the Father will reach down an enormous hand from the firmament, pluck the decadent planet earth from among the stars, and squish it like an overripe tomato.

It's important to mention here that it is the nature of prophecy to be self-fulfilling. Once heard, or otherwise absorbed, a particular prophet's vision can, in turn, shape the vision, the psychology, the choices, and the actions of a prophet's disciples. Having absorbed the specifics of a prediction, most believers in the power of prophecy are entirely capable of going about the business of seeing that a particular prediction comes true—that the transformation they seek does, in fact, take place. That is both a miracle and a curse, because it returns the question of the future to our own hands.

Our recognition of the relative genuineness or accuracy of a prophecy is essentially an afterthought to the process of making it happen. And, divinely inspired or not, that might be put forth as prophecy's chief function. As a species, we're curious about future events not for their value as an objective reality, but as a subjective one. We ask because we want to learn what the future holds, but we also ask because we want to know what we can do about the future—to change, to meet, to escape, or to survive it.

Prophecy, whether served up as a warning or a promise, changes the present because it can serve to change the people who hear it, informing forever their actions and choices, which in turn have the power to alter future events. Individual people can be transformed by the encountering of mystery. Thus, the individual or society is reempowered to cope with the dissatisfactions of the present and to change the future by first changing itself.

Nonetheless, prophecies do come true. Thousands of students of the phenomena are quick to point to the work of the ubiquitous Nostradamus, the work of America's "Sleeping Prophet" Edgar Cayce, and of other mystics, such as Madame Blavatsky, G. I. Gurdjeiff, and in more modern times Jeane Dixon and Ruth Montgomery as irrefutable evidence that prophets are real, that they know something we don't, and that their messages are not to be disregarded. So be it. But just because a prophet's message resonated in the collective enough to come true once doesn't mean that the prophet will be right the next time. Because the future is always in question and the question is always one of choice. And if that much can be said about the future, it can certainly be said about the present and even the past. If our history of prophets and prophecy is "real," it is because we made them real.

However the following messages may resonate spiritually, there is still, in my own opinion, a case to be made for healthy skepticism. Prophecy is expressed in symbolic terms, and symbolism is a flexible language. When we attempt to pin a prophecy down as an absolute, we miss the point and lose our power to shape our world.

The following three sources of prophecy are perhaps the most perennial in our history. I discuss them here not to discourage or to encourage the reader to jump on the mystical bandwagon, but simply because of their immense popularity. Each speaks to each of our three visions of the future and each in its way has served to inform the prophetic collective of those who came after them. These three are long dead, their prophecies uttered in circumstances far different from our own, yet their validity for our own age remains.

These prophets are not so much presented for the value of the message, but for their essentialness to the prophetic tradition that has evolved in our time.

I attempt, when I can, to put the work of a prophet or a particular prophecy in historic, prophetic, and symbolic context. My intention is not to belittle the inclination to prophesy or the message, only to suggest that many of these "predictions" come out of an identifiable context. Many "divine" inspirations have been known to rise up out of some decidedly earthly influences—that doesn't make them wrong. And if a prophet's message or vision is applicable to the contemporary world, it could perhaps be due to the fact that the world does not always change very much over time, despite our collective yearning otherwise.

St. John of Patmos and
The Book of Revelation 80–90(?) A.D.

St. John's (not to be confused with John the Apostle's) terrifying account of the End Times has informed the last two thousand years' of prophecy with a treasure trove of collective mythological imagery. While some may argue that the imagery contained in the Book of Revelation is not mythology at all, that it is to be taken quite seriously as a vision of what is to come, these are the same people who read the Bible as a literal document rather than as allegory. I can add little to that debate that has not already been said. What we do know is that the apocalyptic imagery contained in the Book of Revelation has become an inescapable part of our symbolic vocabulary, just as it was no doubt an inescapable part of its author's. The Book of Revelation is resurrected every time there is a crisis in history. Its significance as prophecy has become, over the years, both predictive and retro-active—if only by virtue of its honored place in our religious and social history. Nostradamus read Revelation, so did Cayce. So have a long line of saints and visionaries through the ages. The imagery of Revelation became part of their visions and concepts of Judgment, just as it was part of John's, whose vision was doubtless informed by the kind of prophetic imagery as is found in the Old Testatment and ancient classical mythology. His seven angels, for example, may well be related to a very old idea that there are the seven circles or spheres of existence, an idea that continues to surface in modern prophetic literature such as *Michael for The Millennium* by Chelsea Quinn Yarbro.

For the record, the Church has never attached the Book of Revelation to any specific date or turn of century. In fact, they have studiously avoided doing anything of the kind. There is currently a lively debate surrounding the predictive/retroactive aspects of the Book of Revelation indicating that our great Tribulation may have already passed some centuries ago. The Antichrist, or the sign of the Beast (666 in Hebrew numerals), bears quite a resemblance to the Latin spelling of none other than St. John's contemporary (and principal oppressor), the Emperor Nero. Still, whether you believe the theory that

John's Revelations were a diatribe against his own
enemies or a prediction of the times to come, there are
passages in the work that cannot fail to give us pause.
It is clear in reading the Book of Revelation that
John's vision was real. He saw something. The question
is—what?

> . . . The sun turned blood red and the stars in the sky
> fell to earth. . . . The sky receded like a scroll rolling
> up and every mountain and every island was
> removed from its place. Then the Kings of the earth,
> the princes, the generals, the rich, the mighty and
> every slave and every free man hid in caves and
> among the rocks of the mountains. They called upon
> the mountains and the rocks. Fall on us and hide
> us from the face of him who sits on the throne and
> from the wrath of the Lamb. For the great day of
> their wrath has come, and who can stand?
>
> Rev 6:12–17

> The third angel sounded his trumpet and a great
> star, blazing like a torch fell from the sky on a third
> of the rivers and on the springs of water—the name
> of the star is Wormwood. A third of the waters
> turned bitter and many people died from the waters
> that had become bitter.   Rev 8:10, 11

Is it only coincidence that the name Chernobyl is
Ukrainian for "wormwood"? Or is the great star that
John wrote would poison the waters in fact a predic-
tion of that terrible nuclear accident? Or perhaps his

vision has yet to be fulfilled and the star called Wormwood will come from some other dimension—a wormhole in the galaxy. Or perhaps John's mad vision was due in part to his own earlier overconsumption of a liquor made from wormwood—the same one the French would later call absinthe—which was hugely popular during the Roman Empire. It was highly addictive, highly narcotic, and eventually drove men to madness. Just the kind of "bitter water" a man would dream about while imprisoned in an arid island cave. We don't know.

Michel de Nostredame
1503–1566 (by the old calendar)

Nostradamus, as he is popularly known, is perhaps the most historically famous prophet with the possible exception of St. John, author of the Book of Revelation. His best known work, *Centuries*, was published posthumously after what appears to be a rather thorough editing by his student, Jean Aymes de Chavigny and one of his sons. The title of the work has nothing to do with one hundred years, but is instead a reference to the fact that there were one hundred verses or quatrains in each volume of the work. Apparently, it was Nostradamus' intention to write ten such volumes, making for a total of one thousand quatrains in all. The seventh volume was never completed, and it has been rumored since that it was Nostradamus' intention to add an eleventh and twelfth volume as well.

The prophetic verses were originally written in an obscure style that is a combination of French, Latin, Provençal, and Greek, making translating the exact nature and meaning of their original content a daunting task, to say the least. Add to which Nostradamus feared prosecution from Church authorities as a magician, so he deliberately confused times, dates, and sequences of events. The first publication of his prophecies consisted of the first three "centuries," and part of the fourth. To say, as many biographers have, that his fame spread like wildfire through France and across Europe upon their publication, however, is misleading. Few in France or Europe were literate at the time, and it is probably far more accurate to say that Nostradamus' verses made him popular in the courts of Europe. Since many of the quatrains, at least in hindsight, address the future fates of many royal heirs, popes, and the like, this great favor he found among the educated people of his time was probably as a kind of court parlor game. Anyone who might be able to decipher the obscure text might be able to save their life or otherwise promote partic-ular political interests. In the mid-sixteenth century, court intrigues were the order of the day: poisoning, unexplained deaths of royal heirs, and sabotage were everywhere. Not coincidentally, his work found favor with Catherine de Medici, wife of Henry II, which doubtless also contributed to his fame.

The prophecies contained in *Centuries* were printed in two parts: the first in 1555, the second after the prophet's death in 1568. The authenticity and completeness of the early editions are nearly impossible to authenticate, and so—since we remain unsure of much of the *Centuries'* authorship—it is difficult to ascertain Nostradamus' ability to predict the future. We will return to some of the specifics of his life that doubtless colored his predictions in a later chapter. However, we do know for sure that whatever the relative accuracy of the predictive quatrains, his work has been published and republished in countless editions since. Periods of historical crisis, such as the Reformation, the French Revolution, the First and Second World Wars, and now the turn of the millennium have all given rise to a host of new editions, reinterpretations, and translations, all seemingly apropos to the time. Unfortunately, we have no interpretation of Nostradamus' work that has not been gifted with 20/20 hindsight. The "uncanny" accuracy of his predictions are more the result of seeing ourselves and our history in the mirror of his symbolic verse.

One thing is certain: Whatever Nostradamus' ability to see the future, he was no optimist. His prophecies are fraught with images of destruction. And if we look for the possibility of destruction, we can almost certainly find it in his works. If Nostradamus saw the future at all, it's clear he didn't think much of it.

> The ancient peoples have left behind witnesses of inner silence, radiance, benediction and beauty, and nations of the future will only pass on traces of pain and death. Every new generation develops weapons of destruction more horrible than before. This development you cannot stop because they have become slaves of their own fear.

Or consider the following quatrains, popularly thought to be predictions of the rise of Hitler.

> Beasts wild with hunger will cross the rivers,
> The greater part of the battlefield will be against
>   Hister [*subsequently translated as Hitler*]
> He will drag the leader in a cage of iron
> When the child of Germany observes no law

> A captain of the greater Germany
> Will come to deliver false help.
> King of kings
> His war will cause a great shedding of blood.

It is historical fact that Hitler's attention had been drawn to the works of Nostradamus, and that he incorporated the prophecies into Goebbels' propaganda machine as early as 1930. One has to wonder that if Hitler had not seen himself in these verses, would he have dared to become the Hitler we know? More importantly, if the prophecy had not become part of the Third Reich's propaganda—if Hitler has not arrived on the scene already cloaked in "divine" messages—would we have let him?

And now consider the quatrains variously attached to the turn of the coming millennium:

> In the year 1999 and seven months
> From the sky will come the great King of Terror
> He will bring back to life the great king of
>   the Mongols
> Before and after, War reigns happily.

Or the following:

The great star will burn for seven days
And the cloud will make the sun appear double
The large mastiff will howl all night
When the great pontiff changes his abode

Or the following:

After great misery for mankind
An even greater approaches when the great
    cycle of centuries is renewed
It will rain blood, milk, famine war and disease
In the sky will be seen a fire, dragging a
    tail of sparks

> Excerpts are from *Centuries* by Nostradamus,
> translated by Erika Cheetham, Berkley, 1973.

What do you see when you read those lines? War? Comets? Natural disasters of all kinds? The end of the Catholic church? The rise of fear? Or a new King of Terror? Maybe the choice is still ours.

Edgar Cayce 1877–1945: America's Sleeping Prophet

Like Nostradamus, Cayce originally gained his reputation as a healer, prescribing a host of "natural" cures for various conditions and clients while in a deep trance. A simple man, Cayce was head-injured as a boy, which may in part account for his ability to return to deep, trancelike states almost at will. Whether or not such an injury affected his power to see the future is uncertain. We do know that he did not begin predicting future events until well established in his avocation, and that perhaps such predictive powers arose in response to the nature of the questions he was asked. During the course of his life, Cayce claimed to read the Bible through at least once a year. He gave almost fifteen thousand readings for individuals, all of which were recorded, collected, and perhaps to some extent edited by his aides, since Cayce was reported to have little or no recall of what had transpired during his trances. Among his predictions for the twentieth century that have been proven out are the rise of World War II, which was perhaps not such a leap, given the state of communications and economic unrest in the world of the 1930s. And in fact, similar predictions of the coming war arose from a number of sources worldwide during the same era. Cayce also foresaw the race riots of the '60s, a vision that might also be considered fairly "predictable" to anyone witnessing the deep inequities between blacks and whites in the American South of the same era. Cayce has also been proven wrong for a number of prophecies, some of which are discussed in the following chapter. For now, we shall concentrate on his visions of the future. The truly important thing about Edgar Cayce is that he is the first of the twentieth-century prophets to speak to the essential importance of personal choice in shaping the world to come. He was born in 1888 and came to maturity over the turn of the nineteenth to the twentieth centuries. Exposed as he was to the collective hopes and anxieties of that era in childhood (the last outbreak of millennialism), his prophetic work bears an indelible stamp of the notion of spiritual, personal, and social choice as dynamic, determining forces. And for that reason, his is a vision that may not have been entirely possible, not to mention popular, before the twentieth century.

Among many other things, Cayce prophesied that Russia was the hope of the world. He saw a new consciousness, arising out of the decline of Communism, that would incorporate religious and mystical values in the coming century—describing it as "not Communism—but rather that . . . as the Christ taught—His kind of communism."

Though Cayce saw great changes in store for the world due to earthquakes and other natural disasters—including a great alteration to the shape of the North American continent due to the loss of most of the East Coast, the southern part of the West Coast and California, and a rather sizable chunk of the South—he was no proponent of a coming Armageddon. Instead, the theme of changing the future through the power of individual goodness and constructive personal choices arises time and again in his readings. Though Cayce saw a need for necessary purging in society in high places and low, he stressed further a need for greater consideration for the individual— a world where each of us would be our brother's keepers. Then, he said, speaking of the future:

> . . . Certain circumstances will come about in the political, the economic and whole relationships in which a leveling will occur . . . or a greater comprehension of the need for it."   (1938) 3976–78

Abiding by spiritual law increases, Cayce felt, our chances both for enlightenment and for survival.

> There are those conditions that in the activity of individuals, in line of thought and endeavor, oft keep many a city and many a land intact, through their associations of the spiritual laws in their associations with individuals.   (1932) 310–11

And more succinctly—

> For, as indicated through these channels oft, it is not the world, the earth, the environs about it nor the planetary influences or associations or activities that rule man. Rather does man by his compliance with divine law bring order out of chaos; or by his disregard of the associations and laws of the divine influence, bring chaos and destructive forces into his experience.   (1935) 416–17

Three
...AND MISSES

WHAT HAPPENS WHEN a prophet or a particular prophecy is wrong? Flat-out, unequivocally, indisputably inaccurate? If seeing the future is a kind of cosmic guessing game, then history has provided us with a number of spectacularly erroneous answers. If the art of prophecy is instead a symbolic system of guidance haphazardly provided by a divine source, some prophets and their disciples have clearly been given the wrong directions from time to time. If we are, in studying prophecy, in a kind of grey area of possibility marked only by symbols and allegorical signposts, why pin things down at all?

The curious thing about failed prophecies is that we tend to believe that the fault or reason for the failure lies not with the prophet or the message, but with ourselves—the interpreters of the message. If a prediction doesn't come off as foretold, it wasn't because the information was wrong; it was because we failed to interpret it correctly. If the Messiah didn't show the last time he or she was expected, it was because we were unworthy, mistaken, or otherwise distracted, not because the prophet who promised the appearance was in error.

This last aspect of the situation is perhaps the most interesting in this day and age, because it points to an important factor in the whole human approach to divine inspiration. While we are, as previously discussed, quite unwilling to hold ourselves responsible for inner knowledge, soul quality, or "the divine" within, preferring to take our inspiration in the form of prophets and prophecy, we are quite willing to take responsibility for errors in what we consider to be divinely inspired material. We were ignorant, we failed to understand, we weren't listening or were unworthy, etc.

It may speak to a great advancement in civilization that we have ceased to shoot the messenger, as it were. But that same tolerance may also leave us exquisitely vulnerable to what the Bible calls "false prophets," cultish thinking, bizarre fringe groups, and a number of other philosophical and cosmic rabbit trails in our search for vision and validation. Millennial thinking may be the most current manifestation of that tendency. We dwell in an age where anyone can "channel" anything; we also live in a time where the "enlightened" have poisoned their children's Kool-Aid and immolated themselves on national television based on the word of a "prophet."

It's all very well to say it can't happen here—but it does happen, and with some regularity. In our current love affair with things spiritual we are not especially critical or discerning of the "messages" that come forth as long as they do come forth. And we seem to be getting less critical all the time. Because we have discovered the need to ask the questions, the exact content, meaning, or common sense of the "answers" can become secondary.

Part of the reason for this lack of discernment is that we are, as already mentioned, looking for a prophetic vision that confirms an existing mythological construct of what the future holds. Messages that resonate in our collective mythology are easy to accept, no matter which vision of the future we are espousing at a particular moment in time—survival oriented, naive, or socially superconscious. Another, perhaps even more important aspect of our collective character and memory is that inherent in that memory is the idea of salvation through enlightenment. One must hear and receive the Word in order to be "saved." And when a civilization is uncertain of its survival past a particular date, the adoption of a belief system, whether divinely inspired or not, becomes especially important—if only to have something to cling to. It is also true that in times of social and historical crisis, getting the message—any message—becomes a form of necessary socialization and bonding. We tune into collective mythology because we have failed to tune into each other in meaningful ways. We want to hear that God will change the world, because we are immensely weary of trying to do it ourselves, and we become increasingly willing to listen to anybody who tells us what we want to hear.

Consider that religious movements which were, as little as fifteen years ago, considered cultish and even bizarre have become more or less commonplace. If, for example a young woman ran off to join the Hare Krishnas in 1977, that action was considered worthy of a kidnapping and deprogramming effort. In the few short years left before the turn of the millennium, packing up the family and moving to Idaho on the strength of a channeled vision is hardly worth community notice. In terms of popular perception, the girl who joined the Krishnas in 1977 was "brainwashed." The family that moves to Idaho in 1997 to await the Second Coming makes us wonder if they know something we don't. Why? Because behavior that was once considered a dis-ease of alienated youth searching for spirituality has become epidemic throughout the population. Books dedicated to "The Reenchantment of Everyday Life" are overnight best-sellers. We search for "healing" and "wholeness" in every area in an attempt to shore ourselves up against the possibility of catastrophe. The concept of self-transformation is big business. But it is important to remember that it is a serious business as well.

A third aspect of our dilemma (and arguably the most damning) is that it is also an essential principle of our spiritual legacy and vocabulary that we must put aside individual "will" or "mind" in order to cultivate an openness of soul. The natural receptivity of such a state will both join us together and join us to God or some other, higher plane of existence. In the individual quest, the ego's objections and personal needs must be put aside for the larger good. Having connected, through belief, to the larger scheme— we must eventually surrender our will to the will of whatever god is giving the message. That particular tenet of spiritual doctrine is true of every religion in the world. And it is also what makes cults possible. The surrender of the individual will required is only a question of degree. Having our questions supposedly answered by the god or religion, we become emotionally, mentally, and spiritually invested. Our questions are supposed to stop. And they do. It is part of the cycle of life. Dissatisfactions and uncertainties, which lead to questions about the future and the meaning of existence in general, are answered by connecting to a particular doctrine, philosophy, or prophecy that seems to provide the answers to those questions. The answers we respond to connect us in turn to a larger scheme or a community of believers. It only seems appropriate that the individual will be set aside to contribute to the good of the community that has in effect restored and re-enchanted our sense of self.

While none of that is wrong in principle it can go terribly, terribly wrong in practice. And so, in our search for the future and for transformation of ourselves and our world, it may be useful to identify some prophetic fiascoes, if only as cautionary tales. The following three examples were chosen to illustrate how the central themes of prophecy resonate in the collective and fulfill our need to identify our mythology as fact, than to point fingers at any particular prophet or philosophy. When it comes to the possibility of making our most secret dreams and ancient memories come true, we are all susceptible. And while the skeptics among you will insist that such follies only happen to somebody else—consider the possibility that that someone else might be your spouse, your children, or one of your elected officials.

Perhaps the only real answer then is not to be too quick to align ourselves with the words of a prophet or a particular religious movement at all, at least not to the point where you start signing away real estate. Perhaps the most sensible approach to the coming millennium would be to keep in mind the Lord Buddha's dying words, "Be a light unto yourself."

Johanna Southcott

An Englishwoman named Johanna Southcott rose to prominence as a religious leader at the turn from the eighteenth to the nineteenth centuries in England. A period that, coincidentally, marked yet another peak of millennialist fever. Among other things, Southcott is claimed to have "predicted" the French Revolution and the rise and fall of Napoleon Bonaparte. She gained more than 100,000 followers in the British Isles and throughout Europe. Then, at the age of sixty-four, she claimed she had been impregnated by the Holy Ghost and would bear a child, to be named "Shiloh." This child would become the new Christ figure, destined to rescue mankind from its history of sin. Clearly, this turn of Southcott's prophecies had origins in

Christian mythology. At sixty-four, it was highly doubtful that she was still capable of having conceived a child in the usual way. She thereby could claim, if only by default, an "immaculate" or miraculous conception. Her name for the second Christ, Shiloh, is derived from an ancient word for peace. Despite the fact that the so-called "Second Coming" of Christ had not, up to that point, been purported to take the form of a second bodily incarnation, the parallels between Southcott's miraculous pregnancy and the biblical story of the birth of Jesus were hard to ignore—even though, on the surface of it, it all seems pretty ridiculous. Yet the key to Southcott's success is more readily understood if we keep in mind the simple fact that she rose to prominence and enjoyed much of her notoriety at the turn of a century—that of the eighteenth to the nineteenth centuries. Turns of centuries give rise to all kinds of anxieties about the future, all manner of religious movements, and all manner of plain silliness. What is interesting is that people believed her pregnant with a new Messiah because they were ready for one. They believed her because they needed to believe a savior was enroute. The turmoils of the Revolution, the failure of Napoleon to unify and "save" the world, the squabbles of the Reformation and Counter-Reformation movements threw established religions into question—all of this made the time especially ripe for Southcott's particular brand of fundamentalist lunacy. As far as most people could see, the Divine Way was pretty much the only way out of the mess the world was in. Imminent messianic intervention seemed all but inevitable. Before it was all over, seventeen out of twenty-one doctors agreed that Johanna Southcott was, in fact, pregnant. But when she died, just before the Battle of Waterloo in 1815, an autopsy showed no evidence of a pregnancy, or, in fact, any specific cause of death.

The Rising of Atlantis

Edgar Cayce (among many others) was a great proponent of the Lost Continent of Atlantis. And, in more recent times, Atlantis has been cited as a never-ending source from which countless New Age doctrines and disciplines have been derived. Practices such as crystal therapy, gem elixirs, aromatherapy, certain herbal medicines, space alien interventions, and the like have all at one time or another been traced to the mysterious lost continent. Since legend has it no Atlanteans survived to tell the tale, any information or knowledge that has come down to us from Atlantis has necessarily come from prophets or from channeled spiritual contacts. A third and perhaps the least reliable source of information about Atlantis comes from people who claim to be reincarnated Atlanteans.

Nevertheless, Atlantis continues to thrive in the popular imagination. Reportedly, it was an ancient civilization, advanced far beyond our own, whose mystical (or alien-enhanced), spiritual, and technological achievements far surpassed the wildest imagination. According to Cayce's channeled readings, many achievements of Western civilization were the result of

Atlantean-inspired technology. The pyramids of Egypt, for example, were—according to Cayce—the result of a collaborative effort between Egyptian architects and reincarnated Atlantean engineers. Which is a curious thesis, considering that if such enormous pyramid structures were crucial to Atlantean technology, evidence of their existence on the lost continent would almost certainly have "surfaced" on the ocean floor and been discovered by the countless expeditions that have sought to prove the existence of the lost civilization. In short, if Atlantean technology was in part responsible for the construction of pyramids—if Atlanteans knew as much as they are reported to have known about the spiritual power of certain geometric shapes—it seems pretty weird that they didn't construct any pyramids themselves.

The earliest recorded origins of the myth of Atlantis probably lie in the works of Plato, whom Cayce undoubtedly read. Plato describes two versions of this civilization in two of his dialogues—one that warred with Greece and lost, allowing Greece to become the new cultural cradle of the world, and, in another later work, in which he describes it as the "kingdom of Poseidon." In fact, Plato's Atlantean fables were probably loosely based on another earlier legend—that of a lost Minoan culture on the island of Santorini (Thera), which was purported to have sunk off the coast of Crete approximately 1000 years prior to Plato's first descriptions of Atlantis.

In addition to identifying hundreds of people as reincarnated Atlanteans, Cayce appears to have described the demise of the Lost Continent as some-

thing of a favorite theme in his prophecies. According
to him, the Atlanteans were destroyed by a misuse of
crystal technology. In attempting to garner the power
of the universe by focusing it through crystals, they
upset the ecological balance of the earth, causing
earthquakes, tidal waves, and the sinking of their continent into the oceans. Submerged Atlantean "fire-
crystals," he reported, are responsible for the spate of
eerie disappearances of ships and aircraft in the
Bermuda Triangle. Obviously, the very Greek concept
of man's hubris in dealing with the forces of nature is
not out of place in analyzing these readings, and neither is the element of the dangers of technology, another popular millennialist theme. Earlier in his career,
Cayce said that evidence of the lost civilization could
be discovered in the Pyrenees and Morocco, as well as
in the Honduran islands, the Yucatan, and, especially,
or notably, in Bimini and the Gulf Stream. Even allowing for plate tectonics, that's quite a spread. What he
was probably referring to, at least in part, were the
ruined pyramids of the Maya and other pre-Columbian
civilizations that are still in evidence throughout
Mesoamerica. Still, the evidence of a flurry of pyramid
building in many parts of the world does not necessarily point to the existence of Atlantis, any more
than the building of skyscrapers indicates New
Yorkers can fly. But Cayce took it all a step further
when he predicted that "Poseida will be among the
first portions of Atlantis to rise again. Expect it in '68
and '69. Not so far away!" A diving expedition was
arranged in 1968 to great public anticipation, but
claims of Atlantean discoveries in the portions of

"pillars" discovered in 3000 feet of water proved nothing but a hoax.

At the time he gave his original Atlantean readings, Cayce was probably offering more in the way of a cautionary tale about the dangers of technological power than he was historical fact. In his lifetime, he saw the development of the hydrogen bomb and nuclear power. His "prophecies" about the history of Atlantis were, in all likelihood, allegorical tales of what might happen. They are by no means historical or documented records of what did happen.

Nonetheless, the myth of Atlantis and other lost civilizations continue to thrive in our collective imagination, serving as a kind of cultural and spiritual missing link in the sometimes convoluted history of human evolution. Keep in mind that we have the same basic physical equipment, brain capacity, and emotional makeup that our ancestors did as much as 50,000 years ago. The longevity of the Atlantis legend and others like it might best be explained as a metaphor for the subconscious mind. A world of "lost" knowledge, "submerged" beneath the ocean floor. Disciplines such as meditation, hypnosis, and the like teach us that the subconscious is both knowledgeable and powerful, able to dictate our actions without our ever being fully aware of it. The subsconscious, not unlike Atlantis, contains lots of valuable information.

So perhaps it is worth considering that if the human race has a collective memory of technology and achievement and great civilizations, it is not because there was necessarily a real Atlantis, but that myths like Atlantis serves as powerful reminders that maybe—just maybe—we know more than we think we do.

The fact remains, no physical evidence of the lost continent of Atlantis has ever been found.

Jose Arguelles and The Harmonic Convergence

In present times, much is being made of the End of Time as predicted by the Mayan calendar. According to the theory, the Mayan cycle of time "began" somewhere between August 6th and 13th, 3113 B.C. and will "end" its cycle of 5125 years on December 21st, 2012 A.D. The person largely responsible for the initial publication of this theory is author Jose Arguelles in a book called *The Mayan Factor*. According to Arguelles, the ancient Maya had a system of telling cosmic time that was ostensibly the result of their ability to observe astronomical events and movements from the tops of their pyramids. Though many found Arguelles' elaborate mathematical "proofs" of his theories entirely impenetrable, his ideas nevertheless fired the public imagination, and *The Mayan Factor* was an overnight best-seller.

According to the author, the Mayan ability to tell cosmic time was part of a greater scientific system of "holonomic resonance, as much of the future as it is of the past." What that meant to Arguelles was that the Mayan calendar was coming around to another beginning, and that promised a great world-wide transformation. The book further puts forth the idea that the people we call the Maya were and are extra-galactic beings who transmit themselves from one star system to the next encoded in DNA. These superaliens seeded our earth as it passed through a galactic beam, and some manner of huge transformation awaits us at the end of the beam—in the year 2012. The beam apparently being roughly 5,000 light years from wherever these folks come from originally.

Arguelles urged back in 1987 that "we are at a point in time 26 years short of a major galactic synchronization. Either we shift gears or we miss the opportunity."

The first re-entry point for the Mayan beam was to be on August 16–17, 1987. At that point, claimed Arguelles, "the counter-spin of history would come to a momentary halt" and the "still imperceptible spin of post-history" would begin. Such re-entry would upgrade our evolution, bringing a new hope and zeal into that "ill-fated creature, twentieth-century man."

Among other things, the Harmonic Convergence would awaken us from our cultural trance, grant us free energy and perfect health, remove blockages in our bioelectric fields, and make "conscious the collective dream time." As the time of these wonders came upon us, we would come to understand that UFOs were not mere Unidentified Flying Objects but instead were Unified Field Organizers—the "intelligent release of galactically programmed, psychically active, radiant energy simultaneously attracted to and emanated from Earth's resonant etheric body."

Whatever . . . Arguelles goes on to say that individuals would, after the initial re-entry in 1987, begin to perceive the Mayan presence among us as "an inner light," or as "feathered serpent rainbow wheels turning in the air." The image of the "feathered serpent" is the image of the Mesoamerican god Quetzalcoatl, the serpent god of peace. According to the specifics of Harmonic Convergence, Texcatlipoca, the god of death and destruction, would, at the Convergence, remove his jade mask and reveal himself to be Quetzalcoatl, who by no mean mythological coincidence had left the earth in 999 A.D. and was, naturally enough, due to return.

According to world prophecy, 144,000 sun dancers, filled with light, will bring on the New Age. This number obviously derives from a number of different sources. Twelve thousand from each of the twelve tribes of Israel—as delineated in the Book of Revelation; or Quetzalcoatl's nine thousand times the four seasons times the four directions; or the number specified in the Hopi prophecies as the number of enlightened teachers. Regardless of what prophetic tradition they came from originally, however, thousands and thousands of people from all over the world gathered at various significant points or "geocosmic nodes" on the earth on a Sunday morning, August 16th, 1987, to usher in the beginning of Harmonic Convergence, based largely on the strength of the information contained in *The Mayan Factor*. They converged from Mount Fuji to Macchu Pichu to Mount Olympus to the Great Pyramid. Crowds practiced harmonic toning in Central Park and tent cities rose up in the Dakotas.

And absolutely nothing happened.

Perhaps I would be remiss at this point not to mention an odd coincidence, namely that the word "maya" derives from a Hindu word for the ability to create illusion. Still, the story of the Harmonic Convergence is important because its themes are indisputably woven throughout all millennial thinking. Even at this writing, the notion that the world will end on December 21, 2012, persists, and most likely will continue to persist up until that date has passed into history.

At centuries' ends, we all experience, to some extent:

1. a need for reassurance that as a species we will continue to survive and thrive in our "post-transformative" state—that whether or not the end comes, there is an "afterlife."
2. that some representative of a higher plane of existence is coming or returning to "save" us from ourselves, since we apparently can't quite achieve salvation without some serious help.
3. a deep-seated need to realign myth and historical synchronicity, because, after all, if the myths of the past turn out to be true, our dreams of the future will come to pass.
4. an increased hyper-awareness and hyper-vigilance as we become convinced of the fact that everything is either falling apart or coming together in an ultimate showdown between good and evil.
5. a sincerely felt and expressed need for global "healing"— resulting in a worldwide reconciliation that will replace our current sense of global chaos.

These are only a few themes of the unfolding millennium; there are others. Whether Arguelles was deluded in his theories of intergalactic beings seeding the earth is ultimately beside the point. The real issue is not whether the earth resonates in the cosmos but that his theories resonated in the hearts and minds of an enormous number of people—to the extent that they would gather all around the world in anticipation of such an event. Yet whatever the participants in the Harmonic Convergence believed about what would happen in August 1987, they were, in effect, rehearsing the turn of the year 2000—the end of the world as they understood it. That they completed their rehearsal in the most benign way possible is to their credit. As we will see in later chapters, there are other, far more sinister rehearsals of the end taking place all the time.

Four

THE PROPHETIC PERSONALITY

WHAT MAKES SOMEONE into a prophet? Is it a vision? Is it a personal transformation? Is it some kind of cosmic hole in the head, an open channel through which can come all sorts of information about the future? Despite the fact that there are a host of books, philosophies, and other instructions flooding the marketplace on how to be your own channeler, see the future, or rediscover your "hidden" psychic powers—on the surface of it, prophecy doesn't seem like a vocation anyone would take up voluntarily.

Still, I think it's valid to examine the lives and personalities of prophets for a number of reasons. First, because they have added immeasurably to our history, our religions, and our philosophical traditions. Second, because comparing the biographies of various prophets might show common personality traits or circumstances that give rise to the prophetic impulse. And, third, because the biographical information that is available about people who are prone to prophecy reveals that perhaps not only are the messages symbolic, the point in time at which the messages were given during the prophet's life can have a great deal to do with the content of the prophecy itself.

It should be clear that as a species we share a symbolic language or vocabulary, and that certain aspects of human mythological and spiritual life have surfaced and resurfaced and found continuing response down through the ages. Thus, this storehouse of symbols and allegories might be considered to be our universal language—the real basis for a sense of human community. Whether the Messiah is to come in the person of Jesus Christ or the Lord Buddha or the plumed serpent Quetzalcoatl, there is a universal messianic vision. A vision that has arisen in totally different cultures under totally different influences at totally different periods in civilization. It is, in its essence, a good idea. It is crisis periods in history, such as our own, that tend to make us respond to that idea as one whose time has come.

And there are other such ideas, equally universal, floating around in the collective soup. One of those is the "end" of time as we know it, as expressed in a number of variations on millennial anxiety. Whether the end of time will come when the self-regulating earth goddess Gaia shakes us off like so many fleas, or as a result of a radioactive comet's trail leaking through the hole in the ozone layer, or as a result of God's displeasure, or a New Ice Age, there is the notion of grand-scale destruction that recurs throughout the prophetic tradition. But since wholesale planetary destruction is a difficult pill for this species to swallow, there is an antidote for the nightmare of annhilation — a kind of counter-dream of redemption. And so we have the collective theme of survival by a chosen few — the proverbial "handful" of good people — from whom will come rebirth.

Still, it's worth considering that the symbolic vocabulary that comprises our collective unconscious contains a great deal of individual experience as well. Collective symbols became collective simply because they happen to everybody.

For example, there is a world cultural memory of a Great Flood. It is the Bible story of Noah and the Ark, but it is also part of a number of other religious and cultural traditions all over the world. In a nutshell, this ancient mythical flood gave birth to a "new age" of humanity — a rebirth of the world. Given the imagery, perhaps it is not at all coincidental that we each are born in a "great flood" of amniotic waters, that we are each "born" or "reborn" out of a flood.

Looked at in another way, it is popular to believe in beings more advanced than ourselves who, whether in the form of angels or aliens or the Mother of God, bring us important "messages" about the future and the nature of existence. Generally speaking these beings are smarter and more powerful than we are. It isn't too much of a stretch to view these figures as essentially parental symbols.

Equally universal are stories of the "end" — perhaps arising from the purely organic realization that each of us will die. Stories of the end revolve around uncontrollable events—meteors, earth changes, God's retribution, etc. We are attracted to these descriptions of the end because dying is a reality over which we have no control.

By these examples I don't mean to contend that symbolism boils down to nothing more than a hodge-podge of fanciful descriptions of the individual life. Nor do I mean to imply that spiritual quests all come down to a narrow universe of self. But it is worth considering that when it comes to collective symbols, what we see is what we get. It's difficult to embark on the search for meaning as found in symbolic tradition without "meeting yourself coming back." So perhaps what we find in prophetic visions and predictions are not descriptions of some ultimate objective reality as they are a kind of allegorical map for psychospiritual development. Millennial periods in history are important—just as periods of crisis in any individual life are important—if only because they make us feel the need to get out the maps and look for direction.

As already mentioned, most prophecy is notoriously non-specific in terms of predicting events in chronological time. Far more often, chronological time is imposed on prophecies by interpreters, either through the gift of hindsight or in anticipation of a perceived chronological "event," such as the coming of the year 2000.

One can't help but wonder why. Surely if events like a planetary apocalypse are as predetermined as many seem to think they are, the exact date is known to whatever divine entity is in charge of making it happen. Why not just publicize it? It seems that running a divine message regarding the end of the world in neon lights in Times Square would be a far more effective method of getting humanity to clean up its act than to couch the message in obscure language spoken through a housewife in Queens. You have only to examine the effect of dates on last-minute Christmas shoppers to see that much.

But despite that fact, prophecies and visions continue to be expressed in obscure symbolic language through relatively obscure people. The messages have a curious sameness to them. Yet they seem mysterious and meaningful because those messages are in a kind of symbolic code. They come to us in trance-like language, in puzzling rhymed quatrains or in signs and portents. We know there's something going on, but we have to work to figure out just what it is.

The interesting thing is that, in working at deciphering prophetic code, it's hard to avoid increasing individual "spiritual" understanding and awareness.

Prophecy "hooks" us into the collective because we resonate to certain symbols and themes. We "feel" the truth of a message because it has been expressed to us in terms that bypass conscious or rational understanding. In trying to figure out why we respond, we discover that what we feel is universal. And that what applies to the world applies to the self. Truth is neither objective nor subjective—it is both. It is Truth. In discovering that, we discover what might be called, for want of a better term, spiritual reality. We become part of a system of shared belief; we learn that we operate according to certain universal laws; we gain a sense of non-material existence.

Many of the religions of the world seem to have arisen around the same myths, spiritual concepts, and ideas. Most of the major religions of the world have also been organized around the teachings of a prophet. But just as there are common threads in prophecy, there are sometimes striking similarities in the personalities and biographies of the men and women who become prophets. These similarities are fascinating if only because they are so difficult to overlook.

The biographies of prophets may hold an important key to the function and nature of the prophetic vision. Just as most millennialist visions fall into roughly three categories, people who experience the kind of mystical visions that constitute prophecy can be divided into three groups as well. These categories might be called the naive, the survivors, and the reborn.

In human terms, prophetic visions are representative of a great deal more than literal predictions of future events. Rather, the symbolic description of the fate of mankind contained in prophecy may be a universal allegorical description of the individual journey through life. It's not what the message contains, but what we read into the message that counts. By reading into it we may discover or rediscover the "divine within."

Though that term has been bandied about for centuries, we all seem to require continual instruction in just what it means and how to use it. Thus, we create externalized versions of our inner reality to help us along. If the prophetic vision is nothing more or less than a means of describing ourselves to ourselves through collective symbology it can be considered a kind of highly condensed form of spiritual instruction. It fulfills our inherent and very human need to tell ourselves stories about what is happening to us. That those stories turn out to be real or fictitious is hardly important—anyone's internal reality can manifest itself in actual events. What matters is that the prophets serve to describe for us some otherwise indescribable aspects of human existence, in much the same way art or more conventional religion does.

Seen from this perspective, the human being's ability to "resonate" and respond to a specific version of the story as a "prophetic" vision is much more comprehensible, because they find a crucial element of self-recognition hidden within the symbology. Taken a step further, a startling number of prophetic visions and, indeed, the very lives of the people we call prophets can also be seen as symbolic expressions of human biographical "passages" or life events. So not only is the message resonant in symbolic terms—so is the messenger. It is much easier to relate spiritually to a housewife from Queens as a representative of a burned-out everyman than to neon lights in Times Square.

Obviously, speculations of this kind are enormously hard to prove. And just as our three visions of the future overlap, types of prophet biographies do as well. Yet, if the function of prophecy is not prediction per se, if its function is instead to shake us up and make us think hard about the mysteries, the element of a prophet's biography might be worth adding to the mix. Below are a few examples from each of the three types of prophets along with some speculation about what those examples might mean in the symbolic arena.

The Naive

Some children are susceptible to prophetic visions. One of the best examples is the appearance of the Virgin Mary to three children at Fatima, Portugal, beginning in the year 1916. Lucia dos Santos, aged nine, Francisco Marto, eight, and his sister Jacinta, six, were tending sheep when they were startled by a white radiance in the form of a beautiful young man who identified himself as the Angel of Peace and instructed them to pray. The Angel appeared two more times in subsequent months and was then replaced by another apparition on May 17, 1917. The "lady" did not identify herself until her last appearance four months later, when she said she was the "lady of the rosary," and performed a miraculous light show, bringing the "sun" near the earth before a crowd of thousands. The specifics of the Fatima prophecy are recorded elsewhere, but it includes instructions to pray for peace, the saving of souls, and the establishment of devotion to the Immaculate Heart. Without humanity's working to improve itself, there would come a great destruction. What's curious here is that the Lady's apparition coincided with quite a number of important world events, including the Bolshevik Revolution and World War I. What's even more curious and rarely recorded is that, of the three children who witnessed the apparitions, Francisco could see them, but not hear or respond to what they were saying. Jacinta could both see and hear them, but could not speak. Only Lucia could see, hear, and respond to the visions. And of the three children, only Lucia would survive to adulthood.

Similar descriptions of a "Lady" appearing to children are found in a record of Beauraing, Belgium, between November 29, 1932, and January 3, 1933. The five children involved were from two different familes and ranged in age from nine to fifteen. The purpose of this series of apparitions was also to instruct the children to pray and to encourage them to get a chapel erected so that people would make pilgrimages to the spot. Given the geographic location vis à vis the rise of Hitler's Germany in that year, the request is fascinating. It is also fascinating that of the five children only the eldest, a girl of fifteen, did not share in the children's last collective vision. Instead, she was singled out for a separate apparition and given instructions to "Sacrifice yourself for me!"

Since ordinary children would not be generally considered to have a vested interest in setting themselves up as prophets, the authenticity of the visions themselves is hard to dispute. It is also hard to dispute the relevance of the "divine" messages in light of world events at the times in history these apparitions appeared. But what is interesting is that though the content of the messages themselves is perhaps less than spectacular in revelatory terms, the messengers and how they reacted to these events can be interpreted as its own allegory for how human beings react at various levels of "spiritual" awareness. Some see, but do not hear or respond. Some see and hear and still do not respond. Those who can do all three evolve into adulthood. In the apparitions at Beauraing, on the other hand, the oldest child was denied the group vision, but given a personal one, with the attendant instructions to sacrifice the self (or ego) to the larger good.

These two groups of children had some other important aspects worth discussing. At Fatima, the children were shepherds, sent out while still very young to conditions that put them in touch with a "natural" environment and also placed them in relative isolation from the rest of the "world" and its distractions. In addition, they had the requisite education in religion to be able to "believe" in what they saw. Simplicity, naiveté, and isolation, coupled with an education in faith, made the conditions for revelation, if not possible, then certainly more probable than they might have been elsewhere.

At Beauraing, the children were older, more "worldly," and had a reputation in their community for not being especially "good" children. In fact, their own parents denied until months into the phenomena that the children saw anything at all, insisting that such mischievous children as theirs would surely not be "chosen" as divine messengers. Nevertheless, they apparently were. These messengers had "evolved" from their naive counterparts at Fatima. They were older, more sophisticated, and less innocent. They were not considered especially "good." And the eldest, the one nearly on the brink of adulthood, was denied the group vision, but given a personal apparition and an admonition. In effect, as an emerging individual, she experienced real conflict with her spiritual role.

Allegorically speaking, we can see an evolution in the naive messenger as represented by these two groups of children. The "lady" that appeared to each group was interpreted by them to be the "mother" of god. The first group was younger and more innocent, in a more bucolic or natural environment. The second group was older and more rebellious, even to the point of experiencing some conflict from its oldest member. In the space of twenty years, the naive messengers had grown up somewhat. Most interesting of all, there haven't been any records of miraculous apparitions of this nature to children since. From a strictly interpretive point of view, perhaps we have collectively gone past the point where the naive can be considered an effective messenger for the divine. As we approach the millennium, innocence has come to be equated more with mere escapism than with actual purity.

The Disillusioned/Converted

There are a host of prophet biographies that point to a history of failed careers, jobs, and marriages before an individual prophet "discovered" his or her true calling as a mystic. Nostradamus and Edgar Cayce are two examples of this group. Alienated though they might have been, most prophets from this group made some attempt to "play it straight" before having had the necessary conversion experience (or rebirth) to become a prophet. There is further evidence of an evolution within the individual prophetic career. The prophetic biography of disillusion/conversion tends to run something like this:

While the gift of superior insight may manifest early in childhood, it is subsequently repressed until some critical or traumatic event in adulthood causes it to surface. Metaphorically, one could describe this as the idea that original insight is "lost" or repressed as the child experiences a period of necessary socialization and maturity. There follows a period of trial and error until the prophet discovers or is converted to his "true" nature—i.e., adolescence and young adulthood bring us to the point where we gain confidence through a variety of experience. Identity begins to emerge.

Generally speaking, the resurgence of prophetic gifts or superior knowledge manifest themselves after a "peak" experience of some kind. Marriage, birth, or a change of location are only a few examples. As is clearly illustrated in the biography of Edgar Cayce, psychic knowledge or insight will manifest initially as the ability to "do readings" for close acquaintances. Just as Cayce did, the prophet or mystic will "graduate" to another spiritual level—usually some manner of "healing." Adults manifest spirituality in nurturing and healing. They have the necessary wisdom to recognize wholeness and reintegration as a goal.

Finally, many prophetic biographies include a period of extensive travel or "exile" or imprisonment in the prophet's life. The period of wandering or exile usually signals another graduation in spritual awareness that in turn will change the character of the message usually involving a de-emphasis on individual readings and a concentration of vision upon world events, catastrophes, or transformations. In terms of the human life cycle, personal wisdom becomes the ability to see patterns and causal relationships. Older adults concern themselves with issues of transformation as death becomes more imminent. In seeking to give life greater meaning, the individual examines the whole.

Nostradamus, for example, was born to a family that converted from Judaism to Catholicism by the time he was nine years old, making him something of an outsider from the start. His education was encouraged by his grandfathers, both Jews, and his subsequent pro-phecies were greatly influenced by Jewish occult literature. He is reported to have been deeply interested in scientific theory and astrology and even agreed with the Copernican theory that the world was round. But his youth and subsequent worldview was also undoubtedly influenced by two significant historical factors. The first was the Inquisition and the second was the Black Death. If his prophecies are full of apocalyptic vision, it could be said that he certainly knew the ropes. The world was quite literally falling apart before his eyes. In fact, Nostradamus began his career traveling throughout France dispensing his own herbs and cures for this terrible pestilence. He gained quite a reputation as a healer. Due to that reputation, he married well and settled in a town called Agen.

But when the plague returned, he was unable to save his own family. His life and reputation in ruins, he returned to a life of wandering. It was during this period of self-imposed exile that his flashes of prophetic insight began to manifest. And it can certainly be said that Nostradamus wrote what he knew—fear, pestilence, and persecution. His visions of the future did not appear to have taken on their apocalyptic fervor, however, until near the end of his life. After publishing a yearly almanac and a series of milder *Prognostications,Centuries* was written in his last eight years of life.

One has only to observe the world to discover that claiming oneself as a prophet is an invitation to have one's life story examined in considerable detail. Yet our fascination with biography, celebrity, and prophecy may very well be a healthy curiosity. If we are willing to examine the lives behind the messages and doctrines that continually confront us, perhaps we will discover key similarities between others' spiritual journeys and our own.

Five

THE NEW BREED

IF WE CAN ACCEPT THAT prophets tend to fall into patterns of evolution roughly concurrent with human stages of growth, awareness, and development, then it might behoove us to take a look at how prophecy's content has evolved in the face of the turn of the coming century. As previously mentioned, we are everywhere confronted with doomsayers, spiritual seekers, and purification movements of every ilk and possible variety as we march toward the year 2000. There are those who want to save the world and those who want to burn it down and those (presumably in the majority) who simply want to survive this momentous turn of the calendar page. But for all the prophets, false and true, who have risen up in our midst to enlighten the clueless masses, it would appear, at first glance at least, that the general content of prophetic messages has changed very little since the last turn of the millennium. Believers are still the chosen, defilers will be destroyed, and The End, as was originally written in the Gospels of Matthew, will still come "like a thief in the night," meaning that nobody is really quite sure.

One significant factor in the evolution of prophetic messages, particularly in the current age, is, of course, in their secularization. Where once recognizable religious visions and symbols were the hallmark of divinely inspired messages, specific religious symbols have been replaced by more culturally recognizable icons. This is not in itself especially surprising, considering the general falling-off of organized religious worship, but it is nevertheless significant, particularly since so many among the brethren seem to have a pronounced inability to recognize the precepts, prophecies, and values of "dat ole time religion" when it's decked out in flashy designer clothes.

But these purely cultural icons and symbols are not to be discounted either, because in the modern world it is popular culture rather than religion that provides us with necessary context. Common cultural values are every bit as much a system of shared belief as Hinduism, Catholicism, or Islam. The benefits of shared belief systems are numerous, yet every such system imposes restrictions as well. Those who fail to perceive or to understand those restrictions are either criminals, insane, or both. In a multicultural society like ours, however, problems arise because there is a greater degree of diversity involved in secularized symbols of cosmology.

The Hindus dealt with this problem by coming up with a set of deities that embodied ideas and aspects of opposites, i.e., the goddess of fertility is also the goddess of destruction. In fact, Eastern cosmology as a whole tends to be much more at ease with the incorporation of this kind of opposition within their gods. Impulses toward both contemplation and conflict dwell more or less comfortably in one divine being, while both carnality and asceticism reside in another.

In the Western monotheistic tradition, however, this dual nature of gods and men is much more difficult to absorb. One might even go so far as to say it takes a millennium every now and again to bring it out. Since Westerners have been conditioned to believe not in ambiguity, but in a rather more authoritarian concept of "god's will," our potential and capacity for both good and evil must be expressed in cultural terms and paradigms. And nowhere is this trend more apparent than in the new breed of prophets and prophecy.

This preoccupation with duality—good and evil, virtue and vice, the saved and the damned—has permeated nearly every aspect of our culture as we struggle to reconcile natural ambiguity and diversity with deeply held ideas of "one way" to salvation. And yet, if our shared belief system has moved away from the religious idea of an omniscient, all-powerful god who dictates the fates of man, that god has to be replaced with an equally powerful idea expressed in secular terms. The key to the evolution of what that idea is can be found in the new breed of prophets and spiritual messengers. For the most part, modern prophets and divine messengers are not corporeal beings at all, but rather disincarnate entities coming through human channels, very godlike, for the most part, but definitely not God. There are a number of variations on these "spiritual doubles" we create for ourselves discussed in more depth in later chapters. For now, though, let's concentrate on the messages and prophecies themselves, because they can give us valuable clues to the exact nature of the evolutionary turn of "spiritual life" in a secularized society.

Consider for example, the fashion in "entity created reality" popularized by Jane Roberts in the channeled Seth material, first published in the 1960s. Channeled through Ms. Roberts, Seth is a self-described disembodied spirit who has reached a higher state of spiritual evolution than we humans can imagine. Though he has been reincarnated many times upon the earth, his energy is now too great to be held in a mere physical form. Nevertheless, he continues to drop by to educate us as to the nature of our reality. Over the years, Seth has captured the attention of seven million readers. Simply put, Seth's philosophy states that we create our reality through our thoughts and perceptions—period. There are, according to Seth, no exceptions at all to this rule. A rule that holds equally true for both personal and universal reality. For humanity to absorb and incorporate this principle of cosmology is presumably our next and greatest evolutionary step. But perhaps it is better to let Seth speak for himself. Excerpts from Seth's selected quotes as they appear on his homepage on the World Wide Web follow:

Consciousness is . . . a spontaneous exercise in creativity. You are learning now, in a three dimensional context, the ways in which your emotional and psychic existence can create varieties of physical form. You manipulate within the physical environment, and these manipulations are then automatically impressed upon the physical mold.

Seth Speaks, Session 515

When man realizes that he, himself creates his personal and universal environment in concrete terms, then he can begin to create a private and universal environment much superior to the (present) one, that is the result of haphazard and unenlightened constructions. This is our main message to the world and this is the next line in man's conceptual development. . . .

Seth, The Unknown Reality, Volume Two, Epilogue

According to Seth, our ability to create reality is the essence of our divinity. Even stripped as it is of divine window dressing, the principle is not new, yet is one that perhaps bears repetition in the especially haphazard constructions that would appear to constitute reality in the age of the millennium. Nonetheless, the origins of Seth's central principle are very old indeed. If the universe itself is a physical manifestation of the mind of god, then Seth's message is simply that man is god, capable of creating reality with his mind, just as god did. We could then interpret this to mean that from the standpoint of our collective consciousness, we have moved away from holding god responsible for reality and toward the notion that we ourselves are responsible for the way things are.

What is especially interesting about this message when received by ordinary human beings entrenched in Western culture is that this supposedly spiritual principle is then interpreted to mean that creating and affecting reality is simply a matter of "putting one's mind to it." That if one only changes one's thoughts, life on earth will conform to desire and will begin to happen a little bit more by design and a little bit less by default. A heady notion, and one that at first glance, anyway, seems far more inspirational that practicable. But then, spiritual principles have always been more inspirational than practical, and perhaps that is their true function. To travel through life devoid of inspiration is a pretty dull business indeed.

As messengers go, however, Seth is especially important to any discussion of contemporary prophecy if only because so many like entities with similar messages have appeared since to follow in his cosmic footsteps. Seven million copies is a lot of books, and there are untold numbers more who have read those books and absorbed the Seth principles whether consciously or unconsciously—as knowledge that comes through any number of other, newer "channeled" beings.

One of the channels described in Kathryn Riddall's book, *Channeling: How to Reach Out to Your Spirit Guides*, speaks of a channel she calls Darryl. In preparation for his psychic development, Darryl (as did other channels described in the book) read Jane Robert's Seth material as "preparation." When Darryl was later queried about the knowledge he had gained from his channeling experiences he reported that:

> . . . the basic foundational teaching is that you create your own reality. . . . All physical experiences are the result of what you have been taught to think they are. . . . Therefore I'd say one of the strongest principles to understand is that if you can get in touch with what your beliefs are . . . whether it's a conscious or unconscious belief, it will show you in no uncertain terms why certain things happen in your life.

And, once more, we seekers meet ourselves coming back. Spiritual laws, whatever the source, are used to illustrate basic principles of human psychology.

The entity Ramtha, first channeled by J. Z. Knight in 1977, has garnered quite a lot of public attention in the last decade or so, though the movement itself actually boasts somewhat less than 3,000 official members. The notoriety of Ramtha has undoubtedly been enhanced by the presence of several well-known television and movie celebrities (perhaps our ultimate cultural icons) in the movement. Several, including New Ager Shirley MacLaine, have subsequently left the ranks for undisclosed reasons.

The name Ramtha originated in several of the recorded sessions of Edgar Cayce, and it is perhaps from these that Ms. Knight derived the name itself, as she openly admits to being interested in a number of spiritual and "occult" pursuits prior to her first experience of Ramtha. Regardless, Ramtha professes to be a warrior-like entity, 85,000 or so years old. He reports to have incarnated on the "lost" continent of Lemuria. Like Seth, Ramtha is also disembodied, and has returned through Ms. Knight to educate the masses to what might be called the "law of mentalism," i.e., the role of consciousness in creating reality. Ramtha is (was) a warrior spirit who holds himself up as a personal example of spiritual triumph. According to one of many press releases, he was allowed to "ascend" to a higher spiritual plane because he was a conqueror who had conquered himself. He "preaches" that he has overcome his ignorance, his will, and his baser desires, and can teach his followers to do the same. In a nutshell, Ramtha professes that he can teach his followers in a few years the same perspective it took him eighty-five thousand to figure out. In his sessions and audiences, Ramtha has been known to address such things as investment advice, interstellar traffic, and predictions of apocalyptic earth and intergalactic changes.

There has been considerable concern and some equally bad publicity over the fact that Ramtha followers successfully appropriated more than one million dollars in Federal funds to run a non-official, so-called "stress-management training program" for FAA personnel, under the auspices of psychologist and Ramthanite Gregory May. However, reports of repeated humiliations, psychological abuse, and bizarre brainwashing techniques from "graduates" of the program resulted in a number of lawsuits, and effectively closed the experimental program down. Among other things, graduates of May's seminars and so-called "diversity workshops," report incidents of beatings; personal humiliation, sexual abuse, and having to do things such as visit the toilet while tied to each other. FAA air-traffic controllers were routinely forced to run a gauntlet, endure physical groping by opposite- and presumably same-sex participants, and become the object of demeaning comments.

Though Ms. Knight claims Dr. May is merely "one of hundreds" to move to Washington State in order to be closer to Ramtha and his doctrine, investigators have discovered transcripts of conversations between May and Ramtha. Ms. Knight and a team of attorneys, however, insist that May has no close ties to the movement, and ask instead that they "not be haunted by the past" as they are only trying to "move forward." Before the program was closed down, May reported training more than 4,000 air-traffic controllers and other FAA personnel.

Kinda makes you want to take trains, doesn't it?

Whatever the ultimate outcome of the investigation into Ramtha and his movement, one has only to read through the Ramtha material to discover that much of this entity's teachings or "philosophy" tends to come forward in what might best be described as an atmosphere of seemingly benign, and yet insidious, psychological abuse. According to Ramtha, humankind is ignorant, hopeless, and more or less beyond redemption as we stand. Nevertheless we seem have to have two important qualities as far as Ramtha is concerned, and these he considers if not our salvation, then at least a starting point—something he can work with. One is our misery and natural discontent with the condition in which we find ourselves—our unhappiness, as it were—and the other is our curiosity. Beyond that we're fairly hopeless as a species. Willful, ignorant, full of defenses like ego, and downright delusional when it comes to being in charge of ourselves. For it is Ramtha (according to Ramtha) and beings like him, who are responsible for anything that humanity might boast of as a cultural, moral, or even technological achieve-ment in the last ten millennia or so. The rest is pretty much drek.

Comfortingly, of course, Ramtha reassures his followers that there are not a few of these super entities out there, looking out for and watching over us deplorable humans. As he has been quoted in one of his numerous books on the nature of reality, ". . . we are legion." So are the demons of hell, according to the Bible, but, hey—why quibble if the guy's investment advice is sound?

What is significant about Ramtha, whatever the specifics of the movement's agenda, is that this entity "initiates" followers into their own capacity for divinity by showing them how to get rid of the ballast of personal ego, individual beliefs, and ignorance to a level where they can master their humanity and their limitations and "open (our) minds to new frontiers of potential and knowledge." According to Ramtha himself he is "not teaching anything new. I am teaching what already is." What already is, is the idea of the divine potential and capacity in man. Ramtha's "expansion" on the basic principle is that man's personal ideology, his will, his limitations, and desires must all be put aside in order for a person to be able to fully experience their divinity and use their minds to create reality. "Truth," according to Ramtha's home page, "is an experience of philosophy."

Thus, we can see a definite evolution in the content of secular spiritual messages. It is no longer enough to receive the message or truth, we must experience it in a fully subjective way. In order to do that, we must put aside individual will. In short, we can read this message as little more than a newly secularized version of the old religious maxim: Even though we supposedly are endowed with the capacity to create reality just as God did, individual will must eventually submit itself to the will of God in order to be effective in the larger scheme. That Ramtha teaches his followers to "overcome their humanity," then, is not as ominous as it might first seem. All humans have had to "die" in one sense or another before they can join with the mind of God.

Even from a brief discussion such as the one above, it is possible to conclude that any real evolution in the nature of spiritual inspiration that manages to eke down to us from various sources on high is more an evolution in terms than a shift in content. From a strictly prophetic point of view, the newer breed of prophets and prophecy is just as inaccurate as it ever was when it comes to predictions of disasters and cautionary lessons about the uses and abuses of power.

What is changing as we face the coming millennium is our symbolic vocabulary. The shift from sacred to secular descriptions of the cosmos is expressed in the de-emphasis on God the all-powerful, to an emphasis on man in all his divine potential. Not by any means all-powerful, but at least partially responsible for the reality in which he finds himself, and able to correct its worst aspects through the embracing of basic moral and spiritual laws. Secularization and the creation of cultural, rather than religious, icons is by no means a bad thing. What we seem to be doing (and perhaps the most significant aspect of all this), is to be taking those moral and spiritual principles away from the relatively exclusive and lofty realms of the churches and into the streets. We are reconstructing our collective symbolic language to remain relevant to modern life. Consider this simple example of vocabulary in terms of its significance. The privilege of receiving divine information, messages, and prophecy no longer belongs exclusively to madmen, mystics, or the merely repressed. An ability that was once reserved only for "psychics," "spiritualists," and "priests" has been taken out of the realm of the esoteric, or even the traditionally spiritual. Such talents are now attributed to "channelers." The secular and even technical connotation of the term makes it somehow more accessible to modern beings. Spirituality, at least in our descriptions of it, is becoming much more democratic. Not so much a gift as a skill. Anyone can do it, simply by virtue of learning to "tune in."

PART II

RAGE

Six

THE LOSS OF CONTROL

IF, AS THE CURRENT TRENDS in prophecy would have us believe, we "are what we think," then a society or culture could be defined by the things that everyone thinks. Shared beliefs, shared symbolic language, and shared allegory all serve to hold the society together. But there is another element that enters into the picture, particularly in millennial periods of history, when anxieties, fantasies, and mass delusions seem to come out in full force. And that element is not so much an examination of what people think as how.

From a purely evolutionary standpoint, human beings have not changed in the last 50,000 years. As much as we would like to believe otherwise, the turn of the year 2000 marks little more than a drop in the bucket of human evolutionary time, much less planetary time. We have the same needs, the same biological equipment, and the same reactions and feelings that our Cro-Magnon ancestors and perhaps even our earlier primate ancestors had before them. But if you accept that there is a god within, then you must accept there is a demon as well. Opposition defines human nature just as it does the rest of nature. There can be expansion and contraction—yin and yang—chaos and order.

Deep within the center of the human brain, just beneath the "thinking" center of the cerebral cortex, there is a conglomeration of neuron and hormone-producing structures known as the limbic system, a little piece of human evolution that has been with us for not a mere 50,000, but 200,000 years of evolution. Roughly crescent- or horeshoe-shaped, the limbic system is also referred to as the mammalian brain because it is the most developed brain portion in mammals.

In mammals, the limbic system regulates things like body temperature. What it also regulates are the deeply ingrained, organic, and one might even say involuntary reactions involved in the business of survival. Here we discover the big four—the "F" words, those drives that govern not the spiritual world, but the physical one: fight, flight, food, and fornication.

But there is even more to it than that. For while the lower portion of the limbic system is busying itself with survival, the upper portion is busy feeling. Emotions originate in this part of the brain, just as survival impulses do. For this reason, our mammalian brain is also called the visceral brain—responsible for those deep, unshakable feelings and passions we hold so mystically dear. The fact is, simple electrical activity in the lower portions of the limbic system is capable of generating responses and emotions in the upper portions.

From a purely physical point of view then, the emotional and intuitive responses so revered by any number of New Age philosophies and spiritual seekers as the ability to "go with one's instincts" or the "gut feeling" is the intellectual exaltation of a process that is nothing more than an organically predictable response to a particular survival instinct. "Gut feelings" or "instincts" or "extra-sensory sensations" are, physically at least, reproduceable under ordinary laboratory conditions by the electronic stimulation of certain areas of the limbic system. These feelings can and do happen spontaneously as a response to a physical event such as an epileptic seizure. Any number of patients who suffer from the psychomotor type of seizure have reported feelings of deep emotion, ranging from raw, primitive passions to deep, profound insight. Emotions are intimately, perhaps inextricably, linked to our survival mechanisms. And when our survival centers are stimulated by such things as encounters with the unknown, the passage of a year or the passage of a thousand years, emotions and passions come to the fore, because our instincts for survival are activated.

More specifically, we are confronted with another, and perhaps the biggest of all the "F" words that lie hidden within our mammalian brains. And that word (and arguably our principle demon) is fear.

Stimulation of the limbic system can create a feeling of premonition that is hard to shake. Our most primitive fears are closely related to those "F" words. We have a fear of mortality, a fear of starvation, a fear that we will be alone or unwanted, unable to procreate, a fear that we will be forced to flee our homes and families, a fear that the species itself will die. This one "F" word—fear—has a wonderfully symbiotic relationship with all the other "F" responses.

But—and this is a significant "but"—what distinguishes human beings from other mammals are the functions of all the rest of the brain—that big cerebral cortex that surrounds the limbic system. The cerebral cortex constitutes our ability to do more than merely react—it gives us the ability to think about why we're reacting, and gives us an ability to make choices that does not exist anywhere else in nature. It's one thing to know you're hungry—it's quite another to decide what you would like for your dinner. More astonishing still is that this cerebral cortex gives us the ability to choose duck a l'orange over salmon en croute to satisfy our hunger, when the fact of the matter is, our bellies would be equally filled and our survival ensured just as well by a meal of raw carp or fresh-killed mastadon.

But when it comes to that fifth and final "F" word, fear, the choices that must be made in response to that feeling are far more difficult to make. Unlike simple hunger, fear is not solely a physical response, though it can have physical symptoms, such as increased adrenaline. Rather, it is an opportunity for our formidable intellectual capacities to kick in. We try to identify the source of the fear, to search for some explanation for why we feel the way that we do. Because fear is so closely linked to our survival mechanisms, it has a very ancient and very valid feeling to it. Because it is an emotion that is so very strong, we feel it can't be wrong.

Fear, after all, holds tremendous survival value— the world outside the caves from which man first emerged can't have been a very hospitable place. People died all the time as a result of accidents, disease and violence, as well as the occasional helping of bad mastadon. Fear became a coping mechanism, a mode of adaptation, an integral part of who we are.

The word "paranoia" is derived from the ancient Greek, and orginally meant "a mind distracted." Yet perhaps it is more accurate to say that when fear is the response, the mind—with its many and infinite layers of intellectual functioning, its infinite capacity to create—serves as the distraction from the original, visceral fear response. After all, the true paranoiac doesn't think for a moment that he is experiencing fear for no reason whatever. They she know they are being harassed and persecuted; they know the End is Near. They are being followed, the target of a vast conspiracy. Someone—or something—is coming to get them. To a person so disturbed, these delusions are not mere fantasies or speculations. It is knowledge we're talking about here, not emotion. Knowledge and systems of belief arise as a direct result of fixation upon the intellectual need to know the "reason" for why we feel the way we do. Fear presents a problem to solve; and the intellect is our means of solving that problem.

As such, man's intellectual capacity is far more godlike in its sheer capacity for creativity than anything based on basic emotional response.

Paranoiac systems of belief arise, then, as a result of the experience of primitive emotions, not sacred ones. No sooner are primitive emotions experienced than the intellect is called in to explain it all. Fear is only one example of the phenomena. Sexual lust, or the urge to procreate, is another. Whole mythologies, belief systems, and societal rituals have arisen around the idea of romantic love; all of which in turn probably arose in response to the very basic and very eternal case of the hots we all have for one another. The same, as we have seen above, can be said about the eternal search for dinner. In no way is this meant to imply that we would be better off reverting to raw mastadon meat, or being hauled off by the short hairs for a little healthy procreation. Rather it is meant to imply only that what holds true for one primitive bio-emotional response holds true for another, and that the real key to any "divine" in our natures may lie not in the heart or the belly or even in that ill-defined thing we call "spirit," but hidden deep in the wrinkles of the cerebral cortex—that miracle of creative thinking and problem solving we call the mind.

When the emotion is fear, however, the god within can become the demon within in very short order. Typical paranoiac progression proceeds roughly along the following line.

In the beginning, there is the sense that something is not quite right. Ordinary life is not proceeding along ordinary or expected lines, and there is a sense of loss of control over one's personal environment. Suspicion and distrust create a problem for the mind— and the mind finds a cause, a "reason." Having identified the reason results in a new emotion—rage. Rage creates a new problem for the mind: feelings of rage must be validated by conflict. Thus, the problem-solving brain goes to work once more and creates occasions for conflict in the form of various delusions. Left untreated, all of the paranoiac's ideas of reference will serve to confirm the emotions of fear and rage. Such emotions create a sense of isolation (Why are these fools so happy? Don't they know what's really going on?) Since humans are essentially social creatures, this creates yet another problem for the mind to solve: how to justify the emotions themselves and the resulting isolation. The mind responds by imagining things, filling the empty stage by creating new illusions and delusions through projection.

The psychological phenomenon of projection is an unconscious defense mechanism whereby we reject emotionally unacceptable impulses or tensions and project them out into the world as a means of staying connected. In survival terms, it makes ultimate sense. It is far easier to run from an external threat than it is to deal with an internal demon. Because the demon is now externalized, the paranoid is free to do more than simply rejoin society. He can become the center of attention—the target of some all-pervasive conspiracy, for example. When that happens, the paranoid begins to entertain ideas of reference that incorrectly attribute causal events and external incidents to themselves. This sense of being the center of focus reinforces feelings of grandiosity, self-affirmation, and fitness for survival. It increases the sense of power because the paranoid is, in his own mind at least, controlling his world. But, since even the best projections tend to go unvalidated by ordinary reality, those feelings still need to be justified and the mind goes to work again, manufacturing fully-formed hallucinations. Allowed to further deteriorate, the paranoiac's sense of personal power, nurtured by delusions, ideas of reference and hallucinations can eventually sanction their taking action against their enemies—i.e., all the non-faithful who didn't believe or share their views.

Loss of control, fear, suspicion, and rage— reinforced by ideas of reference, delusions of grandiosity, hallucinations, and finally vengeance. It can happen to any one of us, at any time. The demon, which dwells deep in the mammalian brain can rise up at any moment, with only the handmaidens of endless creative thought to attend it.

And, as the individual can go, so can society, because society is comprised of people with the same biological equipment, and the same shared beliefs.

So much of what we see in the world around us as we approach the millennium are different manifestations of a paranoiac response to the fear for survival. The fear itself is ancient and primitive. We can't shake it, so we must justify it. Millennial paranoia is generated by the simple realization that we have ultimately no control over time. Time passes, and when it passes our survival is threatened because life is finite. That knowledge alone is enough to set the limbic system jitterbugging with electricity.

We do not control time. We can mark time; we can try to save time. We can attempt to buy time, plan time, and become wildly efficient one-minute managers. But we do not control time—and there will never be "enough" time to suit us. Control over time, in this society at least, is control over life. It is survival. A momentous marker such as the passage of the millennium serves to remind us that we have no real control, that our lives are just so many drops in eternity's big bucket. Fear, our principle coping mechanism, comes into play.

And the mind, that great, creative, godlike force, follows. It begins to look for the reasons and solve the problems and make the necessary projections and otherwise justify all this primitive railing over the loss of control in our lives. We all have the demon; the passage of the year 2000 has awakened it.

Since thought tends to be creative, there must then arise a set of societal movements and manifestations of our collective mental state in response to this collective fear. It's useful, then, to examine the three principle types of millennialists in light of the collective paranoiac response.

The survivalists, as previously mentioned, look for the answers in the past and traditional types of experience. If survival is the basic need, reasons this type, a return to the basics ensures survival. Besides, they're not bothering anybody—just their enemies.

The naive utopians are the masters of projection and illusion. Fear and rage are not justified, not acceptable. Denying those feelings within themselves, attributing them to other, less enlightened types makes the naive more evolved, more grandiose. Sure, they might be poorly understood, but that doesn't mean they're wrong when they insist that spirit guides have assured them spaceships from a faraway planet are coming to rescue a handful of chosen believers.

Does it?

The purification type of millennialist is a fitness freak, a planetary vigilante, a vegetarian. Survival is simply a question of taking the right vitamins. After all, you don't really have to die if you don't want to. These folks are absolutely in control of their survival, thank you very much. It's the rest of the world that's going down the cosmic toilet. That's why we have to get organized. Clean up our act. Show the world by example just how in control of this death thing we can get. That's why second-hand smoke kills non-smokers, why Chernobyl means they never eat Russian caviar. That's why, when Jesus comes—if He comes—they're going to do their best to look busy.

Just in case.

Seven

COMMON FEARS

CAN IT REALLY BE that simple? Are we all merely afraid to die? Is that what all the millennial hoopla is about? Surely there's more to it than that. . . .

Maybe and maybe not. Certainly a number of common fears can be linked directly to fears for survival, but some other modern paranoiac preoccupations, millennial and otherwise, are a bit more difficult to place. Obviously there are a number of issues bombarding us through the media that are manifestations of our collective anxiety over individual, species, and planetary survival. But whatever the degree of media responsibility for "creating" issues, media coverage exists because something is a hot topic—people are interested; certain issues are especially relevant or meaningful while others are not. Our president was recently re-elected because he promised to "build a bridge to the twenty-first century." With rhetoric like that—who wants to hear about Whitewater?

Still, common fears for survival may not constitute the whole reason for our millennial anxieties. Some things, such as our preoccupation with the "epidemic" of infertility, the hole in the ozone, our fixation on "safety" issues, and the nightmare of possible nuclear disaster are relatively easy calls. The obsession with health and wellness is another survival-related issue, albeit one that has been brought down to a more individual scale.

But what about our fear of crime? Is it simply the loss of possessions that is at the root of the fervor to lock "them" up and throw away the key, or, better still, reinstate the death penalty? Is this, too, a survival-based anxiety—merely the fear that one of us, or all of us, might one day become victims? Is it a projection? Are we attributing our own unacceptable rage onto a criminal population as a means of simply getting rid of it? Or are we recognizing the crime rate as an index of the currents of psychic and social unrest that dwell within all of us? The possibility exists that we are perceiving the criminal population, with its refusal to abide by society's rules, as harbingers of the future world. And perhaps we are so steadfastly refusing to recognize the psychological damage and danger present in many such individuals as mitigating factors because we secretly believe ourselves to be similarly damaged. After all, how can abuse cause someone to kill someone else? I feel abused, but I haven't killed anybody, have I?

Yet criminals as omens of a future society is an idea that doesn't seem to go away. It's a popular theme in futurist movies. Think of *Blade Runner, Mad Max,* and *Escape from New York.* And it is true enough that the fear of those who cannot or will not abide by society's rules is not an unfounded one. As any good paranoid knows, more civilizations have collapsed as a result of social unrest than have from Armageddon or the acts of disappointed gods. Nonetheless, the preoccupation with the crime rate is a sign for many that the lines for some final, definitive battle are now being drawn. Will it all come down to a struggle between the faceless them and us? Or is our preoccupation with criminal activity instead the beginnings of the realization that they *are* us?

Homelessness is another popular theme in today's news broadcasts, and as such may reflect an aspect of collective anxiety. For most people, the homeless represent a deep and abiding fear of displacement in the general scheme. The homeless, we are told, tried to play by the rules—and lost. The high majority have held down jobs, have families, etc., and their current state is the result of some circumstance that was beyond the control of even those who play by the rules—a fire, a bad landlord, an illness. An "unlucky" break of some kind has left them with no place to be. There, but for the grace of god, go most of us. Homelessness reinforces our ideas of vulnerability and uncertainty about the future, and in some cases may give us cause to count our blessings, whether or not those blessings are the results of our actions or even our thinking. Because when one no longer has anywhere to be, they are only a breath away from having no future—nowhere to go.

Drugs are another popular evil, a sort of non-issue that has attained the status of a full-blown societal threat. Though our "War on Drugs" has a precedent in the temperance movements surrounding the turn of the last century, when the principle drug of choice was supposedly alcohol, the idea that drugs and drug use threaten the very fabric of society and not just the unwashed masses is relatively new. Middle-class white children are using heroin in unheard-of numbers, or so the news broadcasts would have us believe; marijuana use is up; cocaine has destroyed the lives of countless businesspeople, housewives, and schoolteachers. We must make war on this threat, close our borders against those who would profit from our suffering and addiction. Even "home-grown" mundane drugs like alcohol and tobacco have attained a new status in evil, threatening our lives, the lives of our children, and innocent non-users everywhere. Though it has been argued that the war on drugs is largely a political creation—a kind of red herring thrown to the populace in lieu of addressing more crucial issues—the general population has responded across the board. What's interesting about our preoccupation with drugs is not so much that it is related to health and fitness issues (or even to the crime rate), but that it reinforces our suspicions. People who use drugs are suspect because drugs facilitate a so-called "escape" from reality. People are getting "high" while the rest of us are slogging along through the swamps of everyday life. Escape is unacceptable not only because it reinforces the nagging suspicion that "somebody, somewhere is having fun," but because it removes the drug-user from the shared belief systems that constitute society. Drugs are therefore representative of chaos and breakdown of societal values.

The next widely held fear that seems to govern much of our psychic life as we approach the millennium is the fear of money. Or, more precisely, the fear of no money—of total and complete economic collapse. The fact is the laws of economics are, for most of us, about as comprehensible as cosmic law. That is, we seem to have a vague idea of how it all works, and are fairly certain of the notion that such laws are more or less immutable, but the gaps in our knowledge tend to leave enormous margins for error. People are "ruined" as the result of simple, even stupid mistakes. Playing with money is playing with fire. It is sheer hubris to think that anyone can do it successfully. We've all been confronted with the knowledge that the old, Calvinist laws of money aren't working. God does not reward hard work with a comfortable income, he (or whoever it is in charge) rewards it with more hard work. Saving for your child's education or your old age in the last couple of decades of the twentieth century is more or less tantamount to spitting into the wind. The other side of the coin, if you'll forgive the pun, is equally onerous. Too much money is evil. Money that comes too easily is tainted. The Boeskys and the Milkens of the world deserved whatever they got, and more. Yet there have arisen no new shared beliefs about money to successfully replace the breakdown of old money values, save our collective anxiety about the national debt. Despite the rosy reports about employment, we are "downsized." Despite the indices of prosperity, we are broke—up to our necks in debt. Some predictions indicate that the interest on the national debt will equal the gross national product by the year 2015. Obviously that can't happen. Still more obviously, many people believe the debt must be wiped out— resulting in catastrophic bankruptcies that will in turn result in the complete breakdown of not only the economic, but the social order as well.

Whether you are disposed to believe such dire predictions, the average person feels they have very little control over their financial lives, despite what "they" keep telling us. Nobody has any "real" money. All we have is the pervading suspicion that somebody or something "out there" is busy taking it all away. That somebody might be the government or the World Bank or the Jews or the Arabs or the Japanese or the credit-card companies or the mortgage people. When it comes to our shared beliefs about money, we know that we have been lied to on some very fundamental level. The power we were promised over our lives and our futures as a result of earning a living doesn't seem to exist. And since it doesn't exist for us common folk, it stands to illogical reason that the whole economic shooting match is nothing more than an illusion, a house of cards based on lies and half-truths. To regain our power in economic life requires, therefore, a complete reorganization of a system we know almost nothing about. The system itself must be purified and simplified so that its benefits are once again available to everyone. And so predictions for the coming collapse abound. And a huge assortment of inspirational and instructional materials have come out in support of our paranoia about money. *How to Prosper During the Coming Bad Years, How to Prepare for World Financial Collapse, Millennium Management, Last Chance for American Business*, and *The Great Reckoning* are only a few examples. The mighty will fall; the rich and super-rich will be punished. And poor men, like the rest of us, may still get to heaven in the end. It's only a matter of time.

The crisis in belief about money can be tied to a larger crisis of values. We have become obsessed with rethinking and reorganizing our values. We are quite busily deciding what has real value in our lives, and which values we consider worthy to bring to the future world. The value debate is healthy, at least in the sense that it can be seen as an attempt to regain control over our lives and our culture. The reasoning behind it being only that we may not be able to control everything—but we can control things like our family life. Despite the fact that many have written at considerable length about the idea that this crisis of values is a symptom of a need to return to an earlier, simpler time, it is my own contention that our fixation on values is not about any particular desire to return to the past. Nor is it a backlash against the complications of modern living. Rather, it is a manifestation of a need to search out those values we will bring to the future world by identifying for ourselves what is truly meaningful in the present one. And so we have lively debates surrounding issues of shifting family values, historical values, the value of hours spent at work or in climbing the ladder versus the value of those spent in leisure activities, etc. The notion of value has even permeated our concept of time itself, as can be seen in the development of buzzwords like "quality" time.

Naturally, there are almost as many variations of these common fears as there are wrinkles in the average cerebral cortex and, with that highly creative and indefatigable tool at our disposal, it is pretty safe to say that new shared fears are cropping up all the time. But no discussion of this sort would be considered complete without adding a final fear to the group. And that is our fear of technology.

Technology is so significant because it represents an externalization of our ability to quite literally become god. Technology is our miracle maker. It has shown us signs and wonders no Cro-Magnon would ever dream about. Technology has also given us nightmares too real to ever be entirely disbelieved in the light of day. And all our basic 50,000-year-old biology cannot help but be ambivalent. Our anxiety about technology reveals, better than any other shared fear, just how uneasy we are about our own capacity for the divine. Technology is all about intellect, it is not about emotion. And if god is to dwell only in the intellect— what about our feelings? Where is our morality? And, God himself forbid, what if somebody gets emotional and presses some crucial button, blowing us all to kingdom come? In contemporary life, many cling stubbornly to the notion that it is technology itself that is causing our monumental problems. The planet is dying because of advances in technology; alien civilizations are showing an unhealthy interest in our world due to our "misuse" of technology. Technology causes stress simply because it's there.

Western civilization has sold us the bill of goods that we may have god within, but that we are somehow incomplete without god with the capital "G." To turn ourselves into gods as we are certainly doing by means of this rampant and irresponsible and miraculous technology can only be an invitation to disaster. We have come too close to godhood without obtaining God's permission. And yet, technology remains intimately tied to our sense of destiny.

Anxiety about technology, this demon, this Frankenstein of our own creation, is by far the most pervasive of common millennial fears. Advances in technology are consistently rejected as creative product, relegated to the realms of cold and unfeeling "science" or, conversely, anthropomorphized to the point of being ridiculous. Computers develop "viruses," not destructive programs—software has "bugs."

Of all the shared fears, technology is the two-edged sword that we carry in our march toward the millennium. Technology is both running our lives and ruining our lives. Technology saves lives as never before, and as such can be the instrument of our salvation, or at least our survival. Technology can "create" life in a test tube; we have machines that can breathe for us, see inside of us, stop life and start it again. We have technology capable of destroying our world many times over in the form of bombs, and we have technology capable of killing it by degrees with chemicals and pollutants. We are even the creators of machines capable of replacing human beings themselves. Since our survival instincts are so much a part of us and since technology has freed so many of us from the more mundane business of survival, the whole business of technological achievement threatens on a very basic level. Our Cro-Magnon emotional equipment is terribly at odds with our twenty-first-century achievements. We view these miracles with both a sense of wonder and of terror, as doubtless our ancestors might have done, coming face to face with Windows 95 or CD-ROM.

To live in a world of technology is to live with both the savior and the boogie man. Technology brings us full circle, face to face with the god of mind. Aware of our own power, we fear that intellect will become the instrument of our destruction unless we find ways to "control" it through our emotions.

And once again, we meet ourselves coming back. Conscience, morality, and choice all come into play because we are trying to restore our sense of control and regain our sense of power over our own capacities. Since feelings are what set the mind to work, finding reasons and solving problems, we can only hope that feelings will keep this god within on a proper leash. We look for ways for our feelings, our consciences, and our morality to restrict these creations before they achieve an identity apart from their creators—us.

Eight

CUT ADRIFT

I WAS ONCE DRIVING across country in the middle of the night. There was a great deal of road construction in the area, and perhaps because it was the middle of the night, or perhaps because I just wasn't paying proper attention, I veered off onto a newly constructed stretch of highway. I don't really recall how long it was or how many miles I had driven before I began to realize that I was the only car on the road. There were no highway signs—no brightly painted lane markers, no barriers. I was on a brand new and completely unmarked highway, unfinished and oddly undefined. I didn't even know if I was still in Missouri or had crossed the state line into Arkansas. There was no way to tell. It was three o'clock in the morning, I was completely alone and about as lost as I could get. All of the usual markers we take for granted on the road were simply not there. The whole experience was eerily disorienting; it was weirdly exciting; and it was scary as hell, particularly when I reached the point where this unmarked stretch of highway simply ended, not over a precipice to be sure, but with a single wooden barrier between the road and no more road. The end of the line. No more pavement—no more of the relative nothing I had just driven through—just a collection of ill-defined shapes that must have been construction equipment hulking in the dark on the other side. There was nothing to do but turn around.

There's a comparison to be made with my end-of-the-road experience and life in the late twentieth century. Little by little, as we move onto the new stretch of road that will take us into the future, the usual markers are disappearing. It is disorienting, it's eerie, and it gives rise to some very real fears that we humans have taken a wrong turn somewhere as we head into the darkness of the unknown.

If culture is a system of shared beliefs—if reality is, as our modern sages insist, created by a consensus of perception—then the loss of certain cultural hallmarks is also shared as the world we know changes and transforms. Culture provides us with necessary context—it is one of the ways in which we make sense of our environment. Describing ourselves to ourselves is a vital part of our existence.

In Jungian terms, an archetype is defined as a "collectively inherited unconscious idea, pattern of thought, image, etc., universally present in individual psyches." Cultural archetypes are part of our collective storehouse of symbols. And the loss or passing or disappearance of certain of those archetypes through the passage of time constitutes a collective loss.

A scholar recently referred to the twentieth century as a century of mourning. Never before in history have our collective cultural losses seemed so great. Great enough in fact to make us fear for the demise of civilization itself. Each passing reverberates through the collective, giving rise to a host of fears, old and new. We are stuck with all the same old feelings, the same old experiences in terms of the human life cycle—but so many of the old cultural symbols of those feelings, the old descriptions of what it means to be human, aren't as valid or adequate as they once were.

Still, this constant shifting and reconstructing of our symbolic vocabulary is absolutely necessary. Without it, we'd all be trying to communicate in cyberspace speaking the allegorical equivalent of ancient Greek.

As some parts of our collective symbology cease to be meaningful, we begin to fear for ourselves. As human beings, our symbols are supposed to be more or less eternal. We have been thoroughly conditioned to believe that that which imparts meaning is duration. On-goingness is essential to our vision of who we are. Without a certain sense of permanence, however illusory, we are deprived of our sense of purpose. If those symbols as have come down to us through literature, art, and history do not prove themselves suitably eternal, if these highest descriptions of human reality, are in the end, rather more ephemeral than not, then so are we.

What modern people, innundated with informa-
tion as we are, fail to realize is that it has always taken
time for new sets of symbols and cultural archetypes to
replace the old ones. But in the face of the millennium,
time is the one thing we're not sure we have. And those
newer archetypes or, more properly, descriptions of
archetypes that we pluck out of the cultural soup,
manage to identify and use to shape our collective
vision seem to continually disappoint us. More modern
archetypes that do emerge seem to lack an "eternal"
quality, that necessary staying power we so require.
And so we are caught betwixt and between, cut adrift
from old symbols and the sense of context they gave us,
and waiting for new archetypes to emerge.

But despite the fact that scholars, iconologists,
culture watchers, and apocalyptics are only too happy
to point all this up as evidence of some ultimate
decline, the fact is we're coming up with new
metaphors and descriptions and additions to the
symbolic vocabulary all the time. We just don't have
any real sense of which of those will survive the test
of time.

To say nothing of the fact that it's hard to take
many of those new symbols seriously. They're simply
too . . . new. Yet they are there. Consider the very
strong possibility that everyone will still know who
Elvis Presley was a hundred years hence. Foolish speculation? I don't think so. Whatever you might consider
the relative merits of Elvis's impact upon the culture,
the impact is indisputably, undeniably there. In the
years since his life and death, the name "Elvis" is
enough to conjure up a whole range of reverberative

reactions in the collective. His devotees recognized it when he was alive—the rest of us are reluctantly but surely being converted. "Elvis-ness" is a state of mind—the man is the kind of icon whose story is every bit as representative of modern culture as Jason and Orpheus were of theirs. And as such, Elvis has made the transcendental leap from biography into mythology. A symbol of humanity far more recognizable and valid to modern minds than Orpheus ever was. And while it is true that we've had an assortment of rock and roll Christ-figures since then—Hendrix, Joplin, and Lennon to name but a few—Elvis was the first. And it is Elvis who will serve us as the archetype in the years to come. And for those who consider, or even hope, "Elvis-ness" is some kind of pop cultural fluke, a merely ephemeral phenomena, or even a passing fad, consider that, hard as it is to believe, the religion of Elvis is already very nearly a half-century old. His history is taught and examined in colleges and universities around the world. You can attribute developments like this to a deplorable decline in education if you wish, but the fact is, like it or not, Elvis is part of the canon already.

But just as newer archetypes like Elvis have a way of sneaking under the fence of the collective consciousness, some other and very celebrated cultural symbols and allegories have disappointed us by their sheer transitoriness as our world and, by association, our collective need to describe experience, changes right along with it. Let's look at some examples.

The generations that followed the end of the Second World War had their vision shaped by the exis-

tence of the Atomic Bomb. The Bomb was big—
the bomb was the ultimate metaphor of destruction—
our collective ticket to kingdom come. We built bombs
and then we built bigger bombs, trying to cover
ourselves against the possibility of somebody else
dropping one on us. For several decades, the Bomb was
integral to shaping our vision of the future. It was the
new sword of Damocles, hanging over our collective
heads. It was the ultimate symbol of destruction and
the ultimate symbol of protection.

But the fact is, the Bomb has pretty much done its
metaphorical work. In the years leading up to the year
2000, we live in an age of peace, we live in an age that
saw the Berlin Wall come down and the Cold War come
to an end. We live in an age where terms like "super-
powers" and the bombs they invented once upon a time
have become largely irrelevant. The Bomb has outlived
its usefulness as a collective symbol because we have
pretty much outlived the Bomb.

But it's important to remember that, like our
old friend Nostradamus, the apocalyptic visions of
the post-war era were informed, at least in part, not
so much by the notion that the world could end with
the press of a button, but by the fact that in many
significant respects, the world already had. The post-
war era saw us faced with some terrible realities: Six
million Jews had been slaughtered; the cities and
countrysides of Europe were laid waste. Families had
lost sons and husbands and cousins in terrifying numbers. And those who returned from the battle returned
forever changed, minus arms and legs and sight and
hearing. We had seen a glimpse of the apocalypse

when they dropped the first bombs on Hiroshima and Nagasaki. Only that great destruction had not come at God's hand—it had come at man's. This was a generation of survivors, afflicted by not a little survivor guilt. And contributing to that guilt was that we were the recipients of a host of new technologies in the aftermath of that war. But the psychic war wounds were as fresh as the physical ones—and they were just as scary. Just because the war had ended did not mean fears of war had dissipated. The entire world was suffering from a form of post-traumatic-stress disorder. It was all too clear that what we had been conditioned to think of as ordinary life had changed forever. Suspicions and mistrust and fear were very real—it was the order of the day. All we had to do was find the reasons why we felt the way we did.

And we found those reasons—we identified our enemy in the communists and the conspiracies and the black lists of the '50s. We found it in the Cold War and the Cuban missile crisis, afraid enough of the future to build bomb shelters in our backyards and to wonder if we would be forced to shoot those neighbors who had not the foresight to build their own. The paranoiac demon within was well nourished and dancing a jig— shaping an apocalyptic vision of the future based almost completely upon the awful reality of the past.

And still—nothing happened. At least, nothing on the scale that we had feared it would.

And so, as the survivor generation began to age, the generation that took its place began to look for a new collective vision, both of the present and the future. At its most hopeful, we found a new metaphor

in President Kennedy, whose life and death, incidentally, will probably not prove itself a cultural icon in
the next century. Nevertheless, for a time, Kennedy
was youth, wealth, and power. He was hope personified. The only problem was that he was mortal. His
subsequent assasination confirmed all of our worst
fears for survival. Yet, even at that, the Kennedy glow
did not abate so quickly: For among other things, he
left a very important legacy in terms of the collective—
the space program.

The possibility of space exploration effectively
provided the culture with a new, if ultimately
metaphoric, frontier. It was a new description of something that spoke to a very old need. Not only could
we once again become pioneers, but our fears of technology could finally be put to rest—our intellectual
powers could at last be reconciled with our emotional
goals—our hopes and dreams of a better life in a
better place. With man's first walk upon the moon
we became, if only for a short time, masters of the
universe. The disappointment came when those first
steps did not go much further.

Still, the ghosts of our past anxieties did not
entirely desert us. They continued to haunt and therefore to shape our visions of the future. Consider George
Orwell's *1984,* with its dark vision of a human population reduced to little more than slaves and ciphers,
living under the ever watchful scrutiny of Big Brother,
a technology gone mad. It was an allegory that had a
huge impact on the culture for many years. The book
was almost immediately introduced into the canon
upon its publication, a cautionary example of what
happens when the most sinister of technological

dreams become reality. "Big Brother" and "1984" instantly became a part of our metaphoric vocabulary. As such, they were a kind of shorthand used to express shared fears of too-rapid technological advance, just as Kennedy and "Camelot" had become part of the psychic vernacular—expressions of hope and confidence for the future that simply didn't require any elaboration. Everyone knew what you meant when you spoke of Camelot or 1984.

None of this is meant to imply that history began with the Second World War, only to point out that our search for collective symbols in art, history, and literature is not only an on-going one, but pretty much a business of trial and error. So many of the symbols we were once inclined to think of as permanent are things that as a culture we have outlived and outgrown. And because the pace of life and communication since World War II have expanded our awareness as never before in our history, symbols are adopted and discarded with what a great many people view as truly alarming speed, robbing us of the sense of permanence we so desire.

But—reality happens. The real 1984 had nothing whatever to do with the fictional one. And when it happened, we were forced to give up a symbol, part of our collective vocabulary. 1984 was nothing more than a fairly ordinary ripple in the great river of time. Still, the nature of the collective dictates that we experience mourning and a curious sense of diminishment until the lost symbol is replaced with something else.

But with so much information, technological miracles, and plain product coming at us from so many different sources, identification of the transcendant is much harder than it once was. When all of the knowledge of the world was written down in a book by a traveling monk and copied by hand by other monks, and those books were passed along through countless generations in secret libraries, it wasn't at all difficult to know that a book was an important, even sacred cultural symbol of shared knowledge (especially if you couldn't actually read). Nevertheless, you believed in the Book. The Book had power.

But when you live in a world and time where there are millions of books, when you couldn't read all of them even if you wanted to, when you dwell in a time where there are talking books and E-books and books on CD-ROM, and a whole lot of people you know are writing their own books on their new word processors, the sacredness of the knowledge contained in any particular book is a great deal more difficult to discern. The old symbol falls away, and we're not at all sure of how to replace it or what to replace it with. We mourn the loss of the old and remain a little lost ourselves while we wait for the new to be revealed. It is no coincidence, for example that the "hot" psychological issues of the 1990s are things like "abandonment" and "grief management" and "recovery." All speak to an aspect of what is going on in the collective consciousness, not merely the individual one. The markers and road signs that have traditionally pointed our way to the future are disappearing and their replacements are not yet in sight.

And reaching into the collective in an attempt to revive old symbols and push old buttons is equally frustrating. It's all very well to compare the AIDS epidemic to the Black Death and point to it as god's wrath upon the unworthy, as some imminent portent of a larger apocalypse, but you just can't make it stick. We cannot pretend we don't know what a virus is or how it works. We cannot pretend to ourselves that there are "good victims" or "bad victims"; our ideas about disease have changed too drastically. We know a germ is a germ.

It entirely possible that the much-touted millennial feelings of "crisis," then, are more about a symbolic crisis than an actual one. While it is true that cultural icons like Mom and apple pie cease to be especially meaningful in describing collective experience when Mom is a corporate executive at IBM and the only person you know who makes apple pies is somebody called Mrs. Smith who lives in the freezer case, in reality it still doesn't mean you don't have a Mom or even that you'll never eat pie again. And while neither the image of corporate motherhood or mass-made pies are especially inspirational, they don't necessarily indicate that life itself is devoid of inspiration, only that we are changing, deriving our inspiration from new and ever changing sources.

The simple fact is that we have outlived the usefulness of so many of our metaphoric descriptions of the future that we have begun to feel that time itself is running out. Our obsession with what the future holds has sent us scurrying to the psychic hotlines, the churches, and the gurus. The old uneasiness rises up— if we are indeed in uncharted territory, driving along an as yet unmarked highway, how long before the road ends, the boat sinks, the planet spins out of orbit? How long before whoever is up there drops the other cosmic shoe?

The fear is ancient, it feels very real. But it still remains for most of us to turn that fear into reality. Our obsession with the future is not so much about wanting to know if the world will end, or when it will end, but about needing some reassurance that it won't. Most of us are quite willing to be wrong about the End. There are others, as we'll see in the following pages, who are not.

Nine

THE RELIGIOUS DEAD

"PARANOIA," once said famed killer and cult leader Charles Manson in a *Rolling Stone* interview, "is just a kind of awareness."

The hard truth of the matter is, he was right. Fear puts the mammalian brain into overdrive—it throws the human being into a state of physical and emotional red alert. The senses are more acute, the awareness heightened. Increased awareness creates in its turn feelings of power and grandiosity, due to the reciprocal relationship between the upper and lower portions of the limbic system—between fear and the other four big "F" words. After all, if your survival is not immediately threatened and all those limbic systems are activated anyway, you can find yourself with a lot of very powerful human drives that are all dressed up with nowhere to go but out.

The paranoid is hyper-alert, hyper-vigilant, and hyper-defensive. These feelings cut them off emotionally from other people, yet, depending on the degree of grandiosity involved, they have real drives to fulfill that require contact with others. For example, the paranoid may consider themselves to be the greatest lover the world has ever known—yet will experience no "love" or even any real connection to sexual partners—those partners exist simply to enhance the paranoid's grandiose vision. Ironically, even though paranoid pathology is in fact, forged by emotional and biological conditions, most paranoids pride themselves on their rationality and objectivity. This "knowing" they are "right" is a bow to the intellect—the god within who has successfully supplied them with all the necessary reasons for being the way they are. Paranoia can make mere mortals feel like gods. And in some cases, a paranoid can even become god—at least in their own minds and those of their followers.

When a Charles Manson or a Jim Jones arises in our culture we have to wonder—how could it happen? Why? The tragedies engendered by these bizarre cults seem incomprehensible. Though society knows—at least on an intellectual level—that it is possible enough for one man or woman to simply go crazy, we are forced to ask ourselves: How can a thousand people go crazy, to die as they did in Guyana? How do you get teenagers to drink the blood of their victims? What makes an entire community set themselves aflame?

These issues are so very significant in the collective sense because they throw our very instincts for survival into question. Survival is the universal human need. Survival instincts will take over when the mind fails, when the emotions are confused, when morality itself has ceased to have any meaning at all. How is it possible, then, that there are those among us who are able to lead their followers away from this most basic need? What is more powerful than the need to survive?

The answer, of course, is religion. The need to worship—the need to attach ourselves to something larger than we are. No matter what we may believe about our individual capacity for inner divinity, we feel ourselves somehow incomplete without an external God or the equivalent in feelings of fulfillment.

Whether that need is the result of our conditioning or is as "hard-wired" into bio-consciousness as those four "F's" is beside the point. The need exists. It that same need that has marched us off to war, gotten us dressed up for church on Sunday, and had us singing around campfires and bonfires and witch-burnings for centuries. We believe because we need to belong. The search for belonging is the search for a larger context for our beliefs—a cause, a god, a star. Religion, any religion, is perhaps best defined as the search for both creation and creator. As believers we find someone or something—to believe in us.

Much has been written about the causes and the effects of cult-like belief in the aftermath of tragedies like Jonestown and Waco. Some insist it is the result of "brainwashing"; some of drug use or poor family life; some of ignorance and, yes, even fear. But the phenomenon can never really be adequately explained in negative or even in causal terms. Though the need for religion might very well be a manifestation of our own deeply ambivalent relationship with the god within, and God or his minions on earth a form of projection of those qualities we still consider unacceptable—spiritual hunger does not always have a readily identifiable cause—or a cure. It is difficult, if not impossible, to explain or understand purely in terms of psychological pathology or even secular cosmology—especially when secular cosmology is in as great a state of flux as it is now. This basic human need for what is conventionally called "spirituality" is at once our greatest strength and our greatest vulnerability. One man's cult is another's community. Religion provides a sense of both social and spiritual identity. When religion goes wrong, we have to ask why.

Though there are great many people who prefer to view religiously-based murders and suicides as the work of the lunatic fringe, malcontents, or the simply stupid acts of the ignorant, misguided, or disenfranchised, in the face of the year 2000 it is simply not possible to completely disown such phenomena as historically or socially insignificant. Though many prefer to think of such things as religious cults, satanic worship, or even serial killers as the bastard children of Western civilization, they're getting harder to ignore. It has become increasingly clear that these terrible mistakes belong to us. That they are—even if we are not quite sure how they are—"homegrown."

By the time he was thirty-five, Charles Manson had already spent twenty-two years of his life in

American jails. Jim Jones was from California; David Koresh had a rock band. Worse yet, their followers were people we knew. They were our neighbors, our children, even our friends. They were people not so very different from the rest of us, anxious only to find some larger meaning in their lives. Anxious only to join with the mind of God. A seemingly good and natural impulse that resulted in terrible and tragic consequences.

But putting tragedies like Waco and Jonestown and Oklahoma City at a safe distance becomes increasingly difficult in the fear-charged atmosphere surrounding the approaching millennium. What was once considered the work of madmen and fools has suddenly attained the status of omen or portent. At its most optimistic, we could see that development as a symptom of increased social responsibility: i.e., "If this society has given rise to a Charles Manson, then we'd better take another look at this society." On the other hand, viewing such events as portentous is perhaps due to the fact that we are simply more paranoid and pessimistic as a culture than we used to be—i.e., "If this society can give rise to a Charles Manson, then this society has had it."

But there is a third, and even more interesting aspect of the whole business, due to the fact that there has been a thoroughly millennialist kind of evolution in both sinister and nonsinister new religious movements all over the world. Specifically, instead of a widening of the gap between traditional and nontraditional religious values, we have witnessed a narrowing of that gap. This seeming homogeneity of belief is arguably a manifestation of our collective suspension of disbelief as we approach the millennial marker. Everyone these days is rather appallingly willing to believe anything—good or bad. No one has any real problem if a nice Roman Catholic chooses to carry magic crystals, or a Baptist takes up aromatherapy. Such departures from traditional dogma are more or less tolerated. Yet it is that very homogeneity of belief that may cause certain individuals to go to further and further extremes in search of an ironclad social, moral, and spiritual identity. In fact, the traditional systems of passing collective and societal values from generation to generation are in flux, if not serious disrepair. And when that happens, the attraction of community grows stronger—yet another form of survival instinct. And in the present day's increasingly homogenous, even confused, sense of context, we view such "extremists" with a greater and greater degree of alarm.

A little less than twenty years ago, Charles Manson's arrest report read, "a.k.a." Jesus Christ. Manson garnered his "family" of youthful followers in California in the '60s and early '70s. His youthful army worshipped him. They believed he was their savior; they would have died for him. But Manson instructed his followers that if they were willing to die, they ought to be willing to kill. And so they killed for Charlie. Members of the family went out on murder raids; sacrificing their victims to the bloodthirsty killer who had become their god—Jesus Manson.

Needless to say, Manson displayed all the psychotic symptoms of a full-blown paranoid schizophrenic. He hated the U.S. government; he hated the Jews; he hated the rich. He saw himself as literally Jesus—not the gentle, martyred, biblical Jesus, but Jesus returned and transformed, the divine agent for the wrath of god. Manson saw himself as capable, with his army of followers, of destroying the world as he perceived it, and then arising as the leader of a new world order. In Manson's own words, "The whole thing's a holy war." Though Manson and his followers were notorious for their use of illegal drugs, including the hallucinogen LSD, it is clear from some of his comments that Manson was high on paranoia itself. He terrorized the Family and he terrorized the population and he fed on the fear he created in others, taking it into himself like a drug. Almost as though fear and the ability to create fear were a kind of magical power.

Perhaps Manson perfected these techniques of transforming reality when he was in prison. He used imagination, i.e., cerebral cortex creativity, to escape the reality of prison life. In fact, he came to love prison. He viewed it as a sort of monastery where he could retreat and escape from the world and be free to project and imagine the entire universe. Through Manson's "god within" he transcended reality. The walls of prison became merely an illusion. When he got out, he was able to enhance illusion through drug use, as well as through the adulation of his following. Eventually all reality became for him an illusion. He no longer experienced any conflict between the natural oppositions in life and nature—good became evil and evil became good. Hitler was God, death itself was life.

But Manson's cult was still all about rage—it was about murder that masqueraded as sacrifice. Family members sacrificed both animals and humans; they drank their blood and danced and performed the murders under a ritualistic auspice. They believed they were making sacrifices to their god.

It's difficult to say what would have happened to Charles Manson and the Family if they had not been caught, or to predict, even in retrospect, whether Manson's condition would have deteriorated to the point where he would have insisted his followers become martyrs, but I doubt it, simply because the times themselves would not have demanded that they do so. That the Family was crazed is undeniable; that they killed for their god is indisputable. But the Family was a cult that was not yet purely militant in its beliefs, for all of their violence. They demanded confrontation with the authorities, it is true, but being so far outside of the social order demanded that. Manson's notion of Christhood was anti-Christhood and, as such, was essentially destructive. No one in society, save for his followers, actually thought he was right.

The idea that the world itself was so far from human redemption that only God can rescue it from evil was not really fully formed as a popular concept in the psychedelic years of the late '60s and earlier '70s, and so it could not be used to recruit and manipulate his followers as part of their ideology.

Yet it is that single and entirely millennial element of the spiritual search that might be said to create the need for martyrs. It is the element of social despair that makes for graduation to the next level of what we are calling the religious dead. It is an evolution from sacrificing others to sacrificing self.

The People's Temple as established by the Reverend Jim Jones boasted over a thousand followers by the time of the massacre at Jonestown, Guyana, in 1978. Of those followers, approximately nine hundred and twenty men, women, and children died by drinking poisoned juice. Those who refused to commit suicide for Jones were murdered by other temple members. The full details of that massacre have been reported elsewhere, but the tragedy was in part at least precipitated by the fact-finding mission of Congressman Leo Ryan and the attempted investigation of and intervention in People's Temple affairs by the United States government. Responding to reports of kidnapping and confinement of members against their will, Ryan and his team were attacked by gunmen upon their arrival. Many of that party, including Ryan himself, were killed.

The confrontation with the authorities was the beginning of Jones's personal Armageddon. Those temple members who managed to escape the massacre report that Jones "rehearsed" several scenarios of both outside attack and suicide for weeks prior to the End. There were midnight raids; there were staged ambushes; there were "games" of Russian roulette, as Jones tested and retested his authority and the loyalty of his followers.

Yet the authorities' suspicions of Jones and the Temple were not unfounded. Things were not at all right within the Temple compounds. Teri Buford's letters to the attorney general, recently released under the Freedom of Information Act, reveal, among other things, that Jones and his hierarchy stole millions from church members. Further, the letters reveal that Buford herself had been "instructed by voices" to cut out her heart anddie for Jones and that she begged "God's forgiveness" for what she had done.

Jones's was a far more militant stance than many of his paranoid predecessors, even in cult religion. To live outside the "control" of government was one of the reasons he moved his temple in the first place. Government was the enemy; government was Satan. And the only way for Messiah Jones to save himself and his followers was to find a way to remove them from Satan's control. But it soon became clear that even that was not enough. They were armed, they were drilled, and temple members were fully expecting an ultimate confrontation with their enemy. Jones prepared them for an ultimate confrontation—and that was what they got.

It must have been clear to Jones that his cause was lost with the appearance of Leo Ryan in Guyana. Yet surrender was unthinkable. The world itself was evil, not the Temple. The only option left was martyrdom.

Martyrdom's purpose in mass deaths and suicides of the kind we saw at Jonestown is twofold. First, it offers the chance of personal salvation and redemption, even though the world, the physical form, and more quotidian connections with life are lost. The martyr believes that in death, we join with the ultimate in "something" larger. Death is the transcendence of conflicted reality. In it, we are reabsorbed into the universe—we become one with God. Second, death sends a message of defiance to the "evil" unredeemed world that remains. And so each martyr's death becomes a kind of prophecy, a message that must not be ignored. Dying is the ultimate attention-getting device—the prophet's last word. The numbers of bodies serve only as testament to the purity of the vision. In a conscience-stricken society, forced to deal with a mass suicide of the sheer magnitude of Jonestown, the religious dead become symbolic, or, at the very least, portentous of a final apocalyptic showdown—if only because their dress rehearsal for Armageddon has been so damned convincing.

Thus, the religious dead serve only to exacerbate our millennial anxieties. First, because individually we share so many of the same suspicions, distrust, and disenfranchisement that gave rise to the extremist movements in the first place, and, second, because we are forced to confront the fact that the kind of apocalyptic showdown prophesied by Jones and his followers is one prophecy that can be supremely self-fulfilling.

The principle evolution in extremist religious cults as we approach the millennium can be compared to a similar evolution in prophecy. It is not so much that the message the religious extremist sends us as a culture changes, it is that our perception of it changes, a perception forged by millennial anxieties, by the unspoken, niggling worry that the "nuts" might be right.

When an individual or even a group of individuals is preoccupied with signs of disaster, of planetary destruction, of the demise of world government and religion, it is of no particular note. When society as a whole is preoccupied with the same issues, collective anxiety can forge the atmosphere for confrontation with anyone who flouts the established conventions of conduct and religion, simply because collective paranoia has convinced us confrontation is inevitable. Put another way, if the nuts are right, the world really is beyond redemption. Since that is an unacceptable idea, society must reassert its social power to either obliterate or to reabsorb the "defectors" from the system.

Unfortunately, that is what happened in Waco as eighty members of the Branch Davidian cult perished in a fire at their compound, while members of the press, agents from the FBI and the BATF, and the rest of the world watched in horror and disbelief.

The Davidians first moved to Waco, Texas, in 1935 and would doubtless have gone unnoticed by the rest of the world if it hadn't been for David Koresh and his uneasy relationship with the Bureau of Alcohol, Tobacco and Firearms. John Baylor, a professor of religion at Baylor University and a Waco resident since 1955, has been quoted as saying that up until February 1993, he hadn't ever heard the religion referred to as a "cult."

That term applied to the Davidians, and the touting of David Koresh as a gun-toting apocalyptic was at least in part a joint creation of the media and members of the Cult Awareness Network, who served as "advisors" and "experts" in the fifty-one-day standoff at Waco.

The authorities had first been "tipped off" by a former Davidian, David Block, who had undergone cult "deprogramming" at the hands of key CAN personnel. They in turn alerted the BATF to the existence of firearms in the compound, which apparently was the beginning of the whole affair. One charge by one man while enduring the best efforts of well-known and highly enthusiastic cult deprogrammers. It is true that a year prior to the showdown, there had been allegations of child abuse at the compound. Yet representatives from both social services and child protection agencies were allowed to enter the compound and interview children and adults alike. They found no evidence to support any allegations of abuse whatever, and left.

In viewing the tragedy of Waco, it is clear that society, as represented by the BATF, the media, and members of CAN were perhaps in a far more apocalyptic mood than were the Davidians themselves. Whatever Koresh's level of personal paranoia or the specifics of his messianic vision, it was forged and brought to a crisis by the authorities. If BATF agents had wanted to arrest Koresh, they could have done so during one of his regular trips to town. But the fact is, Koresh could not have been arrested or charged with anything at all until the compound itself was searched. The agency had no evidence of anything save the questionable allegations of David Block and a number of affidavits supporting the search warrant, all of which used the word "cult" in describing conditions at the compound.

In fact, the BATF tipped off the media before serving the warrant, presumably to provide the masses with another entertaining little circus along the lines of "America's Most Wanted" or "Cops." On February 28, 1993, BATF agents attempted to serve a simple search warrant with more than one hundred agents, tanks, and enough firepower to launch a full-scale military offensive. Not surprisingly, the Davidians had been tipped off about the "raid." In the ensuing gun battle, four Federal agents and six group members were killed; Koresh himself was wounded. This began a fifty-one-day siege that came to involve such highly placed figures as the President and Attorney General Janet Reno before it was all over. The allegations of child abuse and cult worship were resurrected by the media and CAN—pushing some necessary and effective buttons in an anxiety-ridden, hypervigilant public. These buzzwords served to obscure some of the larger issues of the confrontation—namely, that even cult members have civil rights. Further, the right to religious worship is separated from federal and state authority by the Constitution, which incidentally, also guarantees the right to bear arms. At Waco, our collective anxiety overrode all that with the need for confrontation with and conquest over this "extremist enemy." The tragedy is that Koresh was more an illusory enemy than not. Less than one hundred and twenty people lived in the compound, many of them children—more a family than an army by anybody's definition. Left alone, they more than likely would have remained so. Consider for example that during the siege, Koresh allowed thirteen adults and twenty-one children to leave. Investigations of the people who did leave have yielded nothing at all to support allegations of the child abuse or mind control so touted and feared by the authorities and the public. Those who stayed with Koresh stayed by choice—either because they believed nothing would happen, or because they believed that dying among their brethren was preferable to life outside the compound. Either reason is a terrible indictment of the established social and moral order. For Waco and cases like it—Ruby Ridge in Idaho, for example—show very clearly that in the struggle to establish social dominance and to clarify those societal values that will emerge in the coming century, it is not always the paranoids or the prophets who are rushing toward the apocalypse. It can be the socially sanctioned actions of the majority that bring the paranoid's vision of apocalypse to pass.

PART III

THE NEW AGE

Ten

THE RITE OF
PURIFICATION

IN THE PREVIOUS CHAPTER, we identified in mainstream societal terms the narrowing of the gap between traditional and non-traditional beliefs. This new, and historically rare, tolerance is highly symptomatic of our emergence into the New Age. The sheer multitude of beliefs can be seen as a "sign," if you will, that we have already passed the high water mark of millennialism as we understand it—despite the fact that we have not yet turned the calendar page to the year 2000. Though things are by no means sorted out, the past decade has seen some significant, and in my own opinion, very hopeful changes in our world. Homogeneity in belief systems is not a cause for alarm or reason to exert and manipulate social power—extremism is. We live in a country that once shut minorities and minority beliefs completely out of the social system. These days, they are tolerated, if not fully understood. If your neighbor down the hall happens to be a practicing witch, for example, you may not choose to have her over for pizza, but you're not especially hankering to see her burned alive in the public square, either.

In fact, as we stand on the threshold of the millennium, many are celebrating the new "wholeness" associated with the renewal of values that brings together the life of the spirit, the life of the mind, and the life of the body. The notion of apocalypse has begun to be recognized as a sort of collective psychic alarm system. If we do not allow ourselves to believe in such notions, we reason, the apocalypse won't happen. The collective yearning for wholesale transformation, even a destructive transformation, has begun to abate as personal transformation becomes more and more of a possibility.

Collective anxiety, at least in this culture, has given way in many significant respects to a reassertion of feelings of personal control. Though it has been by no means abolished as psychically unacceptable to feel the world is somehow on the brink of extinction, there have nevertheless been some very significant strides made by virtue of that alarm having been sounded in the first place. There are watchdog groups minding the polluters and disdainers of the planet's natural resources. Social and political forces, however insignificant or even foolish they might seem to the pessimist, are in play to protect the rights of animals, of the planet, of children, even of the unborn. Whatever the individual reaction to this plethora of special interest groups, lobbies, and proselytizers, the allegorical implications for the "future" contained in the messages of those groups and causes cannot be discounted. Whatever the future holds, we have emerged from our initial phase of millennial terrors to decide, with characteristic human efficiency, that we can actually do something about it. And whatever the eventual effect of such movements on the larger scheme, that alone is cause for celebration. As a species, as a collective, we are still deeply interested in survival. Most of us cannot and do not count ourselves amongst the despairing and disillusioned, nor among the martyred dead. At least not for the moment. We have totaled up the signs and portents, listened to the bell ringers and even the dirges, and made our decision: Whatever time is left, whatever the future holds—there is still time to do something about it, both individually and collectively.

All change, especially collective change, constitutes some loss; but our losses, at least at this point in time, do not seem particularly overwhelming, simply because new movements, new ways of thinking, and a vision of the future, however hazy, has begun to emerge. Though it might be personally difficult not to sneer at the relative social value of movements like political correctness, such movements are, in fact, an attempt to reconcile old symbols and new ones into an emerging collective vocabulary, even if it might seem at times as though we are throwing out the canonical baby with the bathwater.

What such efforts do demonstrate is an attempt at tolerance for different lifestyles, changing social roles,

and emerging belief systems. That attempt at tolerance was perhaps the first in our collective history,
save for the like movements (free love, anti-war,
etc.) that emerged in the '60s and '70s. However,
those earlier social upheavals were still considered
outside of mainstream social order, the result of a "generation gap," a "youth movement," or drug-induced
hippie visions and dreams. Tolerance, wholeness, and
survival were never before united, much less organized
and expressed as social concepts in quite the way they
are today.

In seeking to emerge into the future, we seek to
first purify the present by removing undesirable
elements and behaviors. The notion of purification
being a necesary predicate to change is a very old one,
and, as we already know, the old concepts are not
easily overcome. It might even been said that we have
departed from a state of millennial paranoia into
one of millennial obsessive compulsion, straining to
overlay fear with ritual, with order, and with an
overdefining of boundaries as well as with the over-
structuring of sensory, emotional, and informational
input. Obsessive compulsion as an ideal of moral
rectitude is deep dyed in our culture; the ghost of
"puritanism" is not long departed from our midst,
if at all. . . .

In purely psychological terms, obsessive compulsion is a response to anxiety, hostility, or despair.
Neo-Freudians define the goal-orientedness, the concentration, and the single-mindedness of the obsessive-
compulsive personality as a reaction to the fear of
being overwhelmed by impulses, specifically impulses

that have been inadequately repressed. The obsessive compulsive, then, seeks to conquer the internal self. By rigidly controlling the impulses that arise from the four "F's"—feeding, fight, flight, and fornication—they conquer fear.

In this culture, paranoids have traditionally been considered crazy. Obsessive compulsives, on the other hand, have been role models. Since obsessive compulsion in its less extreme forms has always constituted more or less socially acceptable behavior, organizations that seek to repress or control the world of the future by controlling the values of the present meet with widespread social acceptance and response.

Thus, we have attempts to "control" pornography on the Internet, or the content and moral messages of television sitcoms. Here is the press release that assures us that women "can have it all"—providing, of course, they work ceaselessly at ritualizing and organizing their time, their lives, their households, offices, and families. Obsessive compulsives have given us the *One-Minute Manager*, and the "Great American Smokeout." Their impulses have resulted in movements like the public passion for exercise, a form of subjugation and perfection of the flesh, and such dubious maxims as "no pain, no gain." With characteristic fervor, obsessive compulsives have turned our attention to diet. We must be fat-free, sugar-free, carcinogen-free. New and unknown substances in food in the form of "additives" must be abolished, and we must eat only "fresh," organically-grown foods. Flesh, in the form of meat, must be also exorcised from our consumptive vocabulary—in doing so, we will become more "spiritual" and "ready" for the coming transformation. Just as the mystics, priests, and the faithful of old confessed, fasted, and subjugated the impulses of the flesh in preparation for "communion"—uniting with God. Sex, if practiced at all, should be "safe" sex, though abstinence is the preferred option. Promiscuity is a crime punishable by death in the form of disease. Obsessive compulsives are further preoccupied with issues such as sexual activity by teenagers and teen pregnancy, seeking, through organized social effort, to abolish both if at all possible.

Obsessive compulsives are the ones who extol the virtues of ending "addictions" in all their forms—to drugs, to alcohol, to frosted brownies and even to other people. They have given rise to "self-help" and popular psychology movements and to "recovery" as well, therapy being an efficient and reasonably "scientific" means of controlling seemingly "uncontrollable" impulses. When such therapy or recovery can be achieved in the privacy of one's own home without having to endure the relative indignity of too much by way of self-exploration, so much the better. The same can be said for medicine—for the advances in preventive medicines and the movements toward "natural" cures.

The principle redeeming social value of obsessive compulsives is that they organize. And the resulting organizations help shape society and its values by introducing shared belief as a means for change and transformation, not merely as a result. Individually expressed, the obsessive-compulsive impulse seeks to impose order on chaos. Collectively expressed, it can and does change the world.

However ridiculous, intrusive, and downright annoying the obsessive compulsives and their infernal organizations can seem, their rituals and causes are essentially purifying. They house the homeless, they get people off welfare, they contributed to nuclear disarmament. They clean up society's messes and are significant instruments of social reform. As anxious and hyper-vigilant as obsessive compulsives may seem, collectively at least, these movements are not movements that express deepening social anxiety about the future but ones that rather seek to move away from anxiety. To wash those unwashed masses, to lead us out of the darkness of rage and violence and into a clean, well-lit, and orderly future.

As such, they are both reassuring and trans-formative. The fact is, we are healthier than we used to be, we are stronger and more physically fit, and we don't use as many drugs. We are more aware of sig-nificant ecological and social factors that impact upon the future and we're doing something about them. Whatever the momentary manifestations of the collec-tive obsessive compulsive impulse, these movements are, by and large, purifying and rather shockingly productive. They are a kind of backhanded way of ensuring our survival. They are about being healthy and hard working and "safe." They are about fitness and longevity. They are about living, not about dying at all. And that is all about hope, not despair.

Eleven

CLOSE ENCOUNTERS

In Search of a Spiritual Double

AT ITS SIMPLEST, spiritual doubles are expressions of the conflict or oppositions that exist in all nature, including human nature. At the ends of centuries or, in this case, a millennium, doubles take on more complex purposes as they serve both as reflections of ourselves and as projections of particular anxieties. Doubles are everywhere. We can find them by studying phenomena like angels or aliens, in exploring the world of the inner child, in so-called "soul mates," and even in our monsters.

The eminent millennial scholar Hillel Schwartz identified three types, or more properly archetypes, of the spiritual double in his book *Century's End*. These are the narcissistic or Freudian type, the Faustian or antitype, and the Jungian, or that which comes out of the collective unconscious. Encounters with each of these archetypes constitute, in Schwartz's view, an encounter with nothing less than Fate itself. In my own view, they are more accurately read as encounters with Self.

The rise of our preoccupation with "doubles" is hardly unique to the end of this century. Schwartz maintains, for example, that when "fatefulness is widely at stake, doubles rise to the occasion." The search for spiritual doubles gave us *Frankenstein*, *Doctor Jekyll and Mr. Hyde*, and *The Portrait of Dorian Gray*. In fact they constitute the main plot of a huge assortment of gothic Doppelgänger novels around the turn of the last century. And doubles were almost certainly at the root of such phenomena as the witch hunts a century earlier, in the 1690s.

In our own century, we have "reinvented" the double once again.

But doubling phenomena is much more than yet another outbreak of poorly repressed fears or public hysteria. In fact, doubles constitute a kind of alter ego. As such, our doubles are here to save us as much as they are here to frighten us. The creation of alternate personalities is a type of survival skill, both a psychological and psychospiritual means of dissociating from an intolerably stressful or threatening reality. Most, if not all, documented case histories of multiple personalities have shown us that this type of disorder usually develops as a result of physical, sexual, or psychological abuse. Alter egos emerge as a means to manage the unmanageable, to explain the unexplainable, and to escape from the unacceptable.

Since the collective personality operates the same way individual personalities do, we find any number of manifestations of the "double image," as we approach our own century's end. It is important to remember, however, that alternate personalities do not develop as a matter of conscious choice or even as pure social pathology. They are instead manifestations of subconscious needs, fears, and the attendant coping mechanisms. After all, even the worst psychosis is defined clinically only as "delusions or hallucinations that are not accompanied by insight." Examining the doubles that arise in our own age may yield some important clues to the collective version of what is currently referred to in the psychiatric literature as "Dissociative Identity Disorder."

We can think of doubles as projections of unacceptable or ambivalent emotions and impulses, reflections of our current collective psychic disorder, and as a part of our continuing search for new symbols to add to our allegorical vocabulary. In examining the nature of these alter egos or doubles as manifest in our world, we may be able to get a better perspective on just what we are thinking of ourselves.

Please understand that, once again, it is not the nature or the purpose of this discussion to debate the "reality" or the actual existence of any of these manifestations, any more than it has been my intention to argue in earlier portions of this book the accuracy of prophecy. Whether actual alien beings with pupil-less, almond eyes and gray-green skin are visiting the earth on medical raids is one of those things I personally would rather not know for sure, any more than I would the exact date of the end of the world.

But an awful lot of people do believe in aliens, and an awful lot more are talking about aliens and still more are willing to believe, if not in the reality, then at least in the possibility of aliens. And when huge numbers of people start examining a particular issue in terms of belief, it has an impact on the collective. By examining our "double" lives in terms of their impact on the culture as symbol and allegory, it may be possible to get a "diagnosis" of the inner life of society.

There are both positive and negative manifestation of doubling throughout contemporary culture. We are reexamining older double images from the last turn of century in the remakes of *Doctor Jekyll and Mr. Hyde* and *The Crucible*. We are looking again at technological hubris and our ability to create "monsters" in *Frankenstein* and *The Island of Dr. Moreau*, and we're coming up with a few new twists in mega-death festivals like the box office hit *Independence Day*.

On what might be considered a more uplifting note, we have a resurgence of "angels" in all kinds of endeavor—rescuing, guarding, warning, and generally going about the business of saving us from ourselves. The more negative images that rise up from the collective unconscious in the form of doubles, we'll save for later discussion. In this chapter, I hope to concentrate solely on "spiritual" or relatively positive doubles and what they express about our search for conversion experience, a renewed sense of value and meaning, and about the future itself.

I use the term "conversion experience" to describe most people's close encounters with otherworldly beings because, in most instances, that is exactly what they are. People speak about their encounters with aliens or angels or even their rediscovery of the "inner child" with an almost religious fervor. According to the testimonials, such encounters, if and when they happen, leave the person involved forever changed in many significant respects—never to be the same again. Psychologically, the conversion experience is actually the result of a need for change and renewal in a person's life and sense of self. However, it is equally important to note that such experiences can also result from overstimulation of the limbic system, through threats, real or implied, to an individual's sense of survival. Hence, we have those "profound" emotional responses to certain limbic stimuli we discussed earlier. The conversion experience, then, is what makes "brainwashing" possible. The destructiveness or relative "sickness" of that response is pretty much a question of what beliefs are involved.

But in either circumstance, the individual is "ready" to believe and to change, for better or worse. And, indeed, the changes induced by conversion experiences are not always negative, and can be quite liberating, for they often result in a renewed sense of meaning and purpose through the experience of shared belief systems, feelings of hope, and enhanced self-esteem.

Three examples of contemporary positive or constructive double imagery are The Inner Child, Angels, and Aliens—that is, beliefs in or encounters with certain extraterrestrial beings, civilizations, and technology.

The Inner Child

Popular psychology has given us what almost might be termed the cult of the Inner Child. The Inner Child is a being that dwells within each of us—a lost, frightened, hurt, or confused innocent who was, at some point or another, forced to repress those feelings. The popular consensus is, unacknowledged feelings are troublemakers—able to wreak all sorts of havoc on adult psychology and behavior, causing otherwise unfathomable "addictions," bad relationships, and an inability to function "normally" as a personality. In order to cope successfully in life, we are told, each of us needs must get in touch with Inner Child, parent it, nurture it, and forgive those who trespassed upon Inner Child's emotional domain in the first place. Above all, Inner Child must be allowed to *Feel*. Unless that which has been repressed gets unrepressed, unless Inner Child is accepted and cherished, we will keep making the same mistakes. In short, the future will be the same as the past.

As a metaphor for unexpressed longings and emotions, Inner Child works for a lot of people. It has served as the foundation for any number of popular psychology and self-help movements. As a collective symbol, however, Inner Child has some important implications.

At its most obvious, the Inner Child double can be seen as a public expression of a longing for innocence. It is essentially positive imagery because it expresses an impulse to both identify the problems of the past and to nurture ourselves into a fuller, better future. Some millennialists, Schwartz among them, have spoken of the Inner Child as expressive of our anxiety about the future and the "wounded child within" as a disorder that allows us to go numb and dissociate from history. Yet, Inner Child–dom has proven itself to be a far more constructive than destructive allegory for growth, renewal, and wholeness. What's interesting is that Inner Child is not the "god within." Inner Child's power over us is emotional power, not intellectual or reasoning power. It is about the culture's acceptance of emotion as a governing force in our lives, yet Inner Child is, after all, still a child.

Allegorically, the movement teaches us that if we are able to acknowledge and accept the discontinuity and dissonance within the self—this division between the god of mind and "emotional soul"—then theoretically at least, it is then possible to reintegrate—the emotional self with the thinking self—the limbic system and the cerebral cortex—the world without with the god within. If we learn to listen to those wounded cries, to hear the unheard voices and attend to unspoken needs, we will then be able to incorporate a sense of hope and turn to the future considerably reassured. And if we are not entirely whole, then perhaps we are at least successfully patched up—with all the necessary deals struck between the inner and outer lives.

Angels

In the last decade or so, the appearance of angelic beings to ordinary folks and angelic intervention in otherwise ordinary lives has risen from the ranks of mere phenomena to the status of major industry. Contemporary angels are interesting in that they can be seen to represent a successful compromise between traditional religious symbolism and mortal longings for transcendence. Like the inner child, angels are also not god—but they are presumably a bit closer to god than are we earthlings. Angels function as God's insurance adjusters—they examine our crises and claims, they serve as guardians for the public safety, and they seem (at least in the press releases) to strive to keep our cosmic coverage up and our premiums down.

But angels have changed a lot since their biblical heyday, when they showed up to terrify simple shepherds with God's pronouncements. As manifestations, they have evolved right along with our perceptions of ourselves. Angel images are complex and ever-changing. Though angels have been referred to by contemporary authors such as the Reverend Billy Graham as *God's Secret Agents*, it appears, through the wealth of ancedotes, books, Internet sites, and testimonials that the secret is definitely out, and that the angels' widespread appearances here on the threshold of the millennium are not merely coincidental.

Titles of angel stories revealed on one Internet site include "When I Needed Hope the Most," "The Rainbow Bridge to Higher Consciousness," and, yes— "The New Millennium." A random sampling of these and other accounts of angelic visitations reveal the following about our angel doubles.

Though many modern angels appear in traditional garb with haloes, wings, and the odd spear, many others are nearly indistinguishable from you or I, save that they are "larger," more "beautiful," and "powerful" than either of us. The witnesses and encounterees with angels, however, are just exactly like you and me. The authors and compilers of the large numbers of angel anthologies out there take special pains to speak to the veracity of their angel witnesses. The people who see angels are invariably reliable, down-to-earth, and readily consent to use their real names. They describe their encounters with angelic beings as "once-in-a-lifetime" experiences— i.e., they are most definitely not pathological liars or spiritual alarmists, despite their experience.

As the angels' appearances have become more diverse, so have their angelic duties. Guardian angels fulfill all their traditional functions, of course, being most especially fond of car accidents and playground perils. But many other and diverse phenomena have also been explained as being the work of angels. Good samaritans, close calls of all sorts (from midnight fires to marrying the wrong guy), premonitions and deathbed conversions—all have been explained by "angelic" intervention. Modern angels have also been known to give relationship advice, sway business deals, do housekeeping and fill the fridge, along with the general practice of all the usual cardinal virtues like healing the sick, comforting the dying, etc.

But from the millennial point of view, angels can be seen as expressive of a positive double image simply because, if they are nothing more than projections of ourselves, they remain projections of our best selves. Angels are like we are—only better. Angels keep us "safe" from all the perils out there, they protect our children (children being another huge theme in the angel literature, by the way, and clearly future-oriented). However diverse and democratic their duties might have become in recent times, angels do good. However commercialized their presence, goodness is still present. These modern angels are powerful, but they are not especially scary. Instead, these angels are beautiful. As projected images, we could interpret this as a sign that our own "divine" inner power has ceased to frighten us or be considered cause for undue alarm. In fact, most modern ancedotes with angels involve a being who is not allowed to "change" anything, only to preserve life long enough for the individual to see the light and change him- or herself. In symbolic terms at least, angel doubles are very much a bridge to higher consciousness, because they can be seen to represent a reconciliation of the mortal and the divine within ourselves through goodness, through help, and through caring for one another.

An enormously popular German film, *Faraway, So Close*, explores yet another and even newer aspect of the evolving angels as a positive double image, and perhaps can be read as another sign that the New Age is in fact already upon us. In the film, the angels who dwell in the black-and-white, invisible, and emphemeral universe long for the richness, color, and diversity of mortal existence. These superior beings, for all their powers, are (or so the script would have us believe) defecting in great numbers and without regret in favor of life in the world. Symbolically, evolution of this type in angels is sign of positive changes in our collective vision. Surely if an angel would forfeit immortality to live among people like us, in a world like ours, there is hope. When heaven comes to earth, life on earth has lost its threat and the afterlife of heaven its charm.

Aliens

The third and undeniably most complex manifestation of millennial doubling is that of the current, if only allegorical, "invasion" by aliens. The explosion of alien and extraterrestrial phenomena on the brink of the year 2000 is indeed so complex that no one has yet to do it justice as psychological, social, or even metaphorical phenomena. But, on the brink of the twenty-first century, aliens might be considered the ultimate double—expressive of as many diverse symbols, intriguing agenda, and opposing intentions as mankind itself. Aliens want to warn us, aliens want to abduct us, aliens want to breed with us, aliens want to spy on us, infiltrate our governments, and poison our drinking water. Aliens want to help us clean up the environment, and aliens have killed their own worlds through pollution and war. Aliens have the power to overwhelm us with superior technology, and yet are concerned about our warheads and need our genes. Aliens want our emotions, yet cannot understand when we react emotionally to their presence. Aliens are going to save us, and they are going to destroy us. Your co-workers and relatives might even be aliens. No one is safe from the alien phenomenon— and no one seems to have a clue as to what it all means.

The more negative or malefic collective vision of aliens and extra terrestrials will be discussed in the following chapter. In the meantime, for those readers who may have slept away the past half century, all alien phenomena, positive and negative, is mercifully marked by a number of agreed upon factors.

The first is that the sightings of unidentified flying objects rose dramatically in the years after the Second World War, presumably in response to the development of advanced weapons of war, the influx of new technologies, and the development of the atomic bomb. Some fighter pilots on both sides of the conflict reported unidentified flying objects in a number of bombing missions, and dubbed them "foo fighters."

The phenomenon comes in when one discovers that such sightings of such vehicles have continued to rise dramatically every year since that war in countries all over the world. New Yorkers, for example, reported over 5000 sightings of unidentified flying objects above the Hudson Valey in the mid-'80s. UFO has become a synonym for spaceship. Whoever they are, whatever they want, and wherever they come from, aliens are very popular.

Though many early sightings of saucer or cigar-shaped aircraft reportedly occurred in the skies above key research facilities and military installations in the western United States, nothing much seems to have come of it all until the supposed crash of one such craft at Roswell, New Mexico, during a thunderstorm in 1947.

The Roswell Incident is to alien phenomenology what the Book of Genesis is to the Bible. It is pretty much where and how "it" all began. The story of Roswell is also the quintessential millennial parable: Knowledge gained, especially technological knowledge, is dangerous. Knowledge lost is nearly always the result of a conspiracy or cover-up. And "the truth" is always resurrected by the handful who "survived" the terrors of the "cover-up." Truth survives in death bed confessions and secret conversations passed down through time over beers and coffee around kitchen tables. Truth is passed on, if only in whispers, from generation to generation. Bit by bit, these first- and second- and third-hand testimonials come together to form a big picture. The past becomes reintegrated; the future is assured.

The ship that allegedly crashed at Roswell was beyond our wildest technological dreams, and, as such, it became a nightmare for beleaguered goverment officials and personnel. They reportedly covered up news of the crash and bullied witnesses into silence, for fear of causing widespread panic, a new war, and possible intergalactic retribution. Rumors have steadily maintained that there were also alien personnel aboard the vehicle, some say even survivors, but none of it has ever been proved.

That which cannot be proved can always be elaborated upon. And so was born our alien double in its myriad of manifestations. The basics of the plot may be as old as the world, but for the first time in modern history we had new characters—and symbols—to illustrate it, and aliens became a part of our symbolic and allegorical vocabulary in a very short time.

Initially however, and perhaps fueled in part by a movie industry well acquainted with the box office success of a host of war movies, our alien doubles were considerably less than benign. These earlier "invaders" were from Mars or Venus, or were the results of "accidents" of radiation. In most of Hollywood's early post-war fiction efforts, alien doubles are "body snatchers" or even "blobs," though there are some robot-like creatures as well. All the plots are pretty much the same. Youthful teenagers (innocence) encounter suspicious phenomena (the unknown). Those who believe must join forces against a skeptical or uncaring establishment personified in the authorities or other parental figures. Those who refuse to believe shortly become dead teenagers. The innocents encounter unexpected disbelief and resistance from the establishment. An attitude that usually turns out to be some conspiracy. In the end only a honest few—only a handful of survivors—are willing to help the now less innocent, but more enlightened teenagers save the world. An old plot line, perhaps, but it kept a lot of people wide-eyed at the drive-ins.

It wasn't until Betty and Barney Hill that aliens made another quantum leap in the collective ideology. Their story of missing time, nightmares, feelings of unidentified stress and depression led to the subsequent recovery of memories of an "abduction" and "medical tests" performed by aliens while under hypnosis. Their story set the parameters for thousands and thousands of similar cases that would follow. From the Hills we also got an agreed-upon image of aliens—the frail, almond-eyed grays that have so populated UFO literature since. (And which, incidentally, bear a notable resemblance to the human fetus.)

But the alien phenomenon really made its final millennial bound with the publication of Whitley Streiber's *Communion* in 1984. As we lost the Orwellian symbol of the future, it was replaced, at least for a time, in the symbolic vocabulary by Streiber's tale of repeated alien contacts and abductions that span generations of families. Contact with aliens became "secret knowledge"—shared between fathers and sons, mothers and daughters.

The generational aspect alone would have been a positive development in the alien double, simply because the concept of generational continuity was reintroduced into the anxiety-ridden atmosphere of the burgeoning alien counterculture. But Streiber knitted up the myth another stitch by presenting his admittedly terrifying, utterly outrageous, and trauma-producing intergalactic buddies as essentially benign and wholly advanced creatures. Creatures who are interested in us not purely as science projects or even breeding stock, but who seek us out for purposes of communion and transformation. If we get "it"— meaning the whole alien deal—we will be saved and transformed for the future. Through the sharing of worlds and minds, we will usher in a New Age.

Post-Streiber accounts of aliens incorporate this transformative aspect, even to the point where *E.T.* became a child's best friend in that thoroughly modern fairy tale. So many people now believe that aliens are really here to trade their superior technology for our "strength" and our "emotions" that even some New Age prophets have climbed on the bandwagon. The ubiquitous Ramtha, for example, insists that interstellar beings are, in fact, worlds seeded by entities like himself, while the entity Michael in *Michael for the Millennium* posits that as many as seventy percent of reported alien contacts are, in fact, encounters with beings like himself.

Still, whether the "alien invasion" constitutes nothing more than a collective fantasy, alien doubles are essentially positive as symbols if only because our notions of aliens have made some very positive steps toward the future. What was once a "blob" in camp '50s movies has become a physically weaker, more intelligent, less emotional version of ourselves, looking for a "home." They are interested in our future and the future of our planet. As such, the alien has not a little potential as a collective evolutionary role model. Better still, if their weakness combined with our strength, their intelligence with our emotions and their superior knowledge with our talent for new technologies, who knows what could happen?

Twelve

THE MONSTER DOUBLE

WE HAVE ALREADY established that, both individually, and as a collective, there's a certain case to be made for the existence of both a "god," or a divine capacity for creative understanding within, and a "demon" within, capable of destruction, exploitation, and fear. Since millennialism as a mindset causes us to look forward with both hope and anxiety as we face the unknown of the future, it also causes us to review the past with both mourning and a sense of history. The object of the game of millennialism, if indeed there is an object, is to somehow find a way to reconcile the past with the future, the good with the bad, the god with the demon.

The language of the collective is the language of allegory, of symbols. It is one of the ways in which we communicate at very basic levels; it's a spiritual shorthand of shared beliefs. As we approach the third millennium, it is clear that we have at least made some progress in the incorporation of new symbols, new allegories, and in new manifestations of doubles—those symbols of our divided selves—our "split personalities." But a look at our angels also demands a look at our darker sides. A brief survey of the negative doubles that populate our conscious and unconscious lives can only reveal that if we have come a long way, baby, there is still quite a distance to enlightenment left to go.

Me-ness

Perhaps the darker parallel to the more positive aspects of the Inner Child movement is a social phenomenon that I will call "me-ness." Me-ness has previously been identified as the "me-generation," but in fact its ideals, goals, and publicly sanctioned narcissism has by no means been restricted to the confines of a single generation. Me-ness is essentially anti-social, though it has many social manifestations. Me-ness is "looking out for number one," and "being your own best friend." The insidious thing about me-ness is that it draws upon social phenomena like the various aspects of the New Age movement— fitness, spiritual enlightenment, and purification— and uses them to encourage self-absorption and preoccupation with utterly mundane issues. Me-people have discovered their Inner Child, meditation, and organically grown vegetables. They exercise, they eat right, they consult the I-Ching. They are constantly "recovering" from something, ridding themselves of toxins, or Feng Shui–ing their living or office spaces. They make pilgrimages, see shrinks, and consult oracles. But they remain essentially the same, unchanged in their narcissistic impulses. Worse yet, Me-people use the precepts of the so-called New Age to sanction their isolation, their sense of superiority, and their inability to connect to a larger reality. If the future is going to be so very different, reasons the Me-monster, why worry about the problems of the present? Me-ness essentially remains outside of the collective while masquerading as part of it. Me-ness is further threatening to generational continuity because of a marked inability to connect to mates or to have children. They are so transformed no one can ever really be good enough.

The monster double in all of this Me-ness is the monster of self. It is a self that refuses to mature and demands perfection in the world before allowing itself any real degree of participation in it. Entering the future must be predicated by an endless process of refinement. Me-ness is therefore stuck in a kind of rut of self-exploration, convinced certainly of the "god" within, but unwilling to sully it in a less-than-perfect world, trucking about amongst the unenlightened and unwashed masses. Finally, Me-ness is the delusion of transcendence. Me-people like and draw upon such ideologies as Karma and reincarnation because it allows them to believe in the future and at the same time dissociates them from making real decisions about the present. Yet Me-ness is terribly judgmental. It is the kind of thinking that dictates that people get cancer because they didn't have a good attitude or simply weren't enlightened enough to be able to avoid it—i.e., as enlightened as Me. Though Me-ness restores a sense of control over the immediate environment, Me-ness is dangerous to the collective if only because it employs the language and trappings of the New Age without any real grasp of its meaning or context.

Satanists

The monster counterpart to the traditional symbol of the angel is, of course, the fallen angel, i.e., Satan and his followers. Instead of attempting to reconcile the god within with the demon, the demon is externalized into outer manifestation. While no one really seems to be sure what it is that Satan worshippers do, exactly, or their reasons for worshipping this darkest of lords, everyone is very, very sure that Satanic cults are springing up in our very own backyards, with all the attendant slaughtered house pets, cryptic graffiti, and implications of chaos and destruction. Worse, Satan worshippers have "powers." They are magicians who can make things go their way. While the actual numbers of people involved in devil-worshipping sacrificial cults is uncertain, satantists being by and large an awfully secretive bunch, it is fairly certain that hapless adolescents, innocent children, and long-standing members of the PTA are all involved.

Though the idea of being in league with the devil has been with us for centuries, the modern Church of Satan seems to have been organized around one Anton LaVey, a self-described black magician. In traditional terms Satanism is cause for anxiety, because its precepts can be so very attractive to anyone feeling a loss of control over or a lack of power in their lives. According to a rather sophomoric and certainly vitriolic manifesto posted on the World Wide Web, the nine major precepts of Satanism do not involve blood sacrifice, cow mutilations, or vampiristic orgies, at least not any that are "ritually" sanctioned or demanded. They are as follows:

1. Satan represents indulgence instead of abstinence.
2. Vital physical existence instead of pipe-dreams of heaven or a better future world.
3. Undefiled wisdom instead of hypocritical self-deceit.
4. Kindness to those who deserve it, instead of love wasted on ingrates.
5. Vengeance instead of turning the other cheek.
6. Responsibility to the Responsible instead of concern for psychic vampires.
7. Man is just another animal on the earth gifted with superior cunning and intelligence, making him the most vicious of all.
8. Satanism represents all the so-called "sins" as they lead to physical, emotional, and mental gratification.

9. Satan is the best friend the traditional church ever had, because he has kept them in business for all these years.

The manifesto, such as it is, goes on to describe Satan as a "hidden force in nature, one that permeates and motivates nature." Indeed, Satan might best be described as the darkest of the anthropomorphized beings that rise up from mankind's collective. Satan is so powerful a symbol because he is so very familiar. Satan is the secret desire—the things we might do if given half the chance. Satan is so dangerous because he encourages us to give up the "false" conditioning of civilization—specifically Christianity. And, by association, to abandon notions of both history and the future. If we live only for the gratification of the moment, necessary context and identity is "lost." Chaos rules.

Thus Satan worship makes for especially good press in millennial times because it pushes very important societal and allegorical buttons. For most of us, it is the choosing of death over life, of personal power over personal sacrifice; and as such, it is seen as the perversion of free will. Further, most Satanist cult stories involve teenagers or children. It is the ultimate kid-gone-wrong story—the ultimate failure of family and of society to impart crucial values and notions of good and evil. In millennial terms, the future is "lost" or at least thrown into jeopardy, not through struggle, confrontation or even apocalypse, but because of simple negligence. We thereby lose the battle between good and evil—the battle of self—

by default. Evil triumphs because we simply weren't paying attention. In fact, Satanic worship and cults have gotten so much attention and what its practitioners feel is unfair press coverage, The Official Church of Satan has put out its own bunco sheet, warning would-be initiates away from evil and dilettante impostors, pseudo-Satanists, and sacrificial charlatans. The true Satanists are very concerned. One of the cautions contained on the bunco sheet says: "Beware of cults offering sex orgies and drugs, or killing animals in the name of Satan. As you well know, these are not part of Satanic practices. The leaders are copying the lame-brain spook stories from Geraldo or Oprah and obviously know less than you do. Use common sense; don't let someone take advantage of you for his or her own perversity; examine motives carefully."

More Aliens

The monster counterpart to the hovering aliens that watch over us from on high are—well—other aliens. Though most of us have made a measure of peace with the frail, diminutive, brutally scientific, yet essentially benign "grays" that populate contemporary UFO literature, it seems even aliens are not without their monstrous doubles. The infamous men-in black, the vampire bigfoot with the alien head called *El Chupucabras*, and the unfeeling kidnappers who steal our ovum and sperm and even our memories for intergalactic zoo exhibits are all out there in force, as is the persistent notion of an on-going conspiracy. As the hit television show assures us, "The Truth Is Out There." It's just that someone, or something, is trying to keep it from us.

Aside from their implications as modern collective symbols, aliens—even monstrous ones—are very important to millennialism because they demonstrate that as a species, we don't quite have the handle on what exactly the difference is between a shared belief or a shared experience and a shared fantasy. Defenders of the "belief" in aliens point to the similarity of experience as evidence of the factual existence of beings from outer space. All abductees, for example, see ships, lose time, have been experimented on and returned to earth, only to have the process repeated.

Belief or disbelief in UFOs and aliens seems to rest only on the "reliability" of the eyewitnesses, and the plausibility of intergalactic space travel. Traveling from one solar system to another is, as far as we know, actually impossible. Yet our love/hate relationship with technology makes us more or less certain that it is at least a theoretical possibility. In theory at least, space is still representative of the frontier—the escape. It is a notion so deeply entrenched in our culture that it is only natural that we would populate that space with superior worlds and superior beings. In reality, space is still an unknown. And while it is unknown, collectively we share the fantasy that everything and anything is possible, including travel.

Most eyewitness testimony concerning the existence of aliens and alien contact with humanity is madeby fairly normal people without discernible ulterior motives. Their experiences are remarkably similar. But then, so are the messages of prophecy, so are accounts of religious ecstasy, and so are stories of near-death experiences.

But shared experiences don't prove that the experiences weren't fantasies. Fantasies and symbols that have arisen as descriptions of universal, not individual experience. We have a cultural memory of the *War of the Worlds;* we grew up watching the same movies and television shows, reading the same books, and playing with the same toys. Just because nearly everyone knows who *Frankenstein* or *The Creature from the Black Lagoon* is doesn't mean that those monsters, in any of their various reincarnations, are real. And no matter how much we'd like to believe otherwise, the fact that methods such as hypnosis are used to retrieve alien abduction and close encounter memories is no indication of their authenticity. The fact is, people are far more suggestible under hypnosis, not more truthful. Hypnosis bypasses the reasoning mind. Suggestibility is what makes hypnosis work; it also makes individuals under the influence of hypnosis more fantasy prone. By accessing the vast wealth of information, symbolism, and memory available in the subconscious or unconscious mind, we may very well be able to access the collective unconscious as well. But our capability for symbolic and allegorical description of experience doesn't make the recollections of alien abductions retrieved under hypnosis real experiences.

Still, aliens as an emerging collective symbol have a great deal to say about the coming millennium and our ideas of the emerging self. They are symbols of hope and self-examination; they are fears of technology and the need for communion. But for all of that, the monster double in this instance incarnates only when we try to attach those symbols to ordinary notions of "proof." Physical proof of the existence of extraterrestrial beings has not surfaced in half a century, nor is it likely to. The truth of alien existence, if indeed there is one, is still "out there" and likely to remain so, until we are forced to examine our aliens in the light of a future reality.

In the meantime, however, there is a unified theory of the alien presence on earth recently put forth by Chris Rutkowski of the University of Manitoba, that may help illustrate the alien conundrum in a newer and lighter aspect. The text of his essay, originally published in *The Swamp Gas Journal,* is reprinted here in its entirety by permission of the author.

THE SWAMP GAS JOURNAL

Special Issue #4   ISSN 0707-7106
Spring, 1996

Alien Incompetency Theory:
A Unified Theory to Expain UFO Phenomena

by Chris Rutkowski

One of the most significant issues in ufology today is the attempt to explain the wide variety of conflicting, confusing, and bizarre elements of the UFO phenomenon. In every subfield of ufological studies, there are aspects that strain the logic of even the most seasoned researcher and cause one to doubt the rationality of the genre.

To this end, a new theory has been developed by members of Ufology Research of Manitoba (UFOROM) which appears to explain most, if not all, of these baffling elements. The theory, labelled AINT, is the Alien INcompetency Theory, and describes how all the confusing aspects can be explained by assuming one simple tenet: aliens are incompetent.

To illustrate the theory, one need only to look at examples from within the phenomenon itself, including its outlying subfields. First, let us look at alien abductions.

One of the basic premises of alien abductions is the conscious recall by abductees of their experiences aboard alien spacecraft. Nearly all abductees report that during their ordeal, the aliens create some sort of mental block within their minds so that they cannot remember what has occurred. Yet, as evidenced by the huge number of abduction accounts published and under investigation, these mental blocks are ineffective.

This is odd, considering the advanced technology and knowledge reported to be held by the aliens. Some abductees report that their captors claim thousands of years of development beyond our own, yet, they, too, have failed to produce a lasting screen memory that can withstand our feeble efforts to unlock it via simple hypnosis techniques duplicable by any charlatan or stage magician. Why would this be?

[Vladimir Simosko, a UFOROM associate and noted Fortean researcher, has suggested some alternatives. Aside from sheer incompetence, he notes two other possibilities: 1) aliens have a wacky sense of humor; and 2) they *want* us to remember, despite the pretense of intending us to forget.]

Another curious observation is that nearly all abductees report aliens with roughly humanoid shapes and comparable sizes, but with different origins and purposes. Some aliens tell their victims they are from Venus, some from the Pleiades, and others from Zeta Reticuli. Since space science has learned Venus cannot support life, this is obvious misinformation. As for the Pleiades, these are stars much younger than our Sun and without hope for planets with suitable living conditions at this time.

Some aliens claim their home planet has deteriorated from misuse and pollution, and wish to warn us about our own disruption of our planet. Others suggest they need our biological materials to breed new life (literally) into their gene pool, perhaps to regain such things as emotions or other human characteristics. It is interesting that these scenarios imply that the aliens have somehow caused their own demise and that without our help they are lost. In other words, they made some serious mistakes. It is not too much of a stretch to suggest they were incompetent in managing their resources!

Of course, some aliens are said to claim that they are superior to us and have their own agendas. This is precisely the claim an incompetent person would make to cover his or her mistakes in order to keep from being embarrassed.

We can look at other aspects of abductions for further evidence. One abductee studied by John Mack described how she woke up one morning after her abduction, wearing lavender underwear. This was baffling to her because she didn't own any underwear of that color. Mack quickly intepreted this to mean that the aliens had somehow made a mistake on board their craft during a busy mass-abduction, and mixed up abductees' clothing. Other abductees have reported returning from their abductions with slippers on the wrong feet and other items of clothing either missing or improperly fastened. In a case studied by Budd Hopkins, an abductee's earrings were found to be in backward after her ordeal on board a craft.

This all speaks to one explanation: the aliens were incompetent. One would hope that superior beings who have been watching humans for many years would have easily picked up nuances such as the color of our clothing and the way jewelry is fastened to our bodies.

Simosko would again note that this could be a display of an alien sense of humor, or perhaps an "intelligence test" of some sort. Regarding further refinements of AINT, he offers four postulates:

1) If the aliens are intervening to "help us along," they are incompetent, because it isn't working out too well; humans remain relatively unsophisticated and not very "tuned-in" to the universe.

2) If the aliens are intervening by holding us back, it isn't working all that well, either, since although an overwhelming majority of humans are tuned-out, there are a number who are attempting to raise the level of consciousness: Mother Theresa, the Pope, Sun Ra, the Dalai Lama, Sharon Stone, etc.

3) If the aliens are trying *not* to intervene, they're even more incompetent than the other postulates would indicate.

4) If there are several different groups of aliens, some helping and others preventing our advancement, this is proof of incompetence because they cannot "get their act together."

Another aspect of the UFO phenomenon is crash/retrievals. Associated with the idea that some alien ships have crashed on Earth is the concept that terran government or military bureaucrats have failed to keep the crashes secret, allowing some documents to be leaked to UFO researchers.

The most famous crash story is that of the Roswell incident, in which a flying saucer apparently crashed during an electrical storm in New Mexico in 1947. While researchers have spent many years tracking down witnesses and speculating as to where the ship might have gone down, the obvious question has never been asked: Why did it crash in the first place? One only needs to consider accidents of terrestrial vehicles in order to realize the answer: pilot or driver error.

It would be truly remarkable to consider that an alien pilot who has navigated his (or her or its) craft through interstellar space using highly advanced technology and propulsion would be unable to maintain level flight through a mere thunderstorm. There is only one reasonable and possible explanation: the pilot was incompetent. Considering the large number of saucer crashes now claimed by researchers, it would seem that many aliens have difficulty flying their vehicles. Surely this could imply that many are incompetent.

We can look to crop circles as further support for AINT. Allegedly, crop circles constitute a form of "communication" between aliens and ourselves. It is implied they are trying to warn us of or prepare us for some upcoming fateful situation through the creation of "agriglyphs," consisting of complex mathematical patterns and obscure symbols. Why would they attempt to communicate with us in such a fashion? Why not just send a radio message or write something in English or Japanese on a sheet of cardboard? Why 100-foot-wide Mayan lettering in marketable durham?

Obviously, their communication skills are less than exemplary, especially since researchers cannot come to an agreement as to the exact messages (other than something about impending "earth changes"). The aliens must be, of course, incompetent.

What about the infamous Men-in-Black (MIBs)? They are described as human in appearance, though possessing some characteristics that give them away. Their facial pallor is often olive or grey in color and their eyes are wide and staring. Their movements are jerky and their speech stilted. They may ask people unusual questions or otherwise show an unfamiliarity with terran customs. For example, in response to the query: "Hey, buddy! What you lookin' at? You want a knuckle sandwich?" an MIB might say, "Yes, please, with some mayonnaise." Such actions easily show they are not humans at all; if their purpose was to mimic humans, their imperfections show that they are, again, incompetent.

Contactees often will share their imparted knowledge from their alien mentors. Unfortunately, practically all contactees claim contact with different aliens from different planets and with different messages to humankind. (They are similar to abductees in this way.) When pressed to ask their channelled entities for more palpable proof of their claims, or perhaps a usable prediction or two, the contactees are told by the aliens that Earth is "not ready" for the knowledge or, instead, give a vague diatribe about "parallel vibrational states" or "temporal matter disruptions."

An examination of other channelled material finds many other examples of alien doubletalk and bafflegab. Rather than accepting the channelled information as revelations from higher beings, the lack of content of the messages suggests something else: the aliens themselves don't know the answers or lack the information as well. Again, we can ask how an incredibly advanced civilization would not be able to give one single example that would prove their superiority. Could it be that they do not know the answers, despite their reputed intelligence?

One can also ask why aliens would choose to abduct people from lower castes or social status rather than those in positions of authority. Why don't they land on the White House lawn? Perhaps they don't know to do so. How could they not know this? They are incompetent.

Even the implants found inside some abductees are curious. Each one is a different size, shape, and/or composition, and while there is a trend for some to be found in abductees' noses, others are found in feet, shoulders, wrists, and knees. Surely, if the aliens are conducting a scientific test, their methodology would be consistent. In fact, the implants appear to be little more than chunks of metal or calcified plastics rather than microtransmitters. Perhaps the alien doctors don't know what they are doing.

In all of these examples, it is possible to interpret the aliens' actions as being far from superior. In fact, they seem rather ridiculous. But, if the aliens are really superior beings from an advanced civilization on a distant planet, why are they acting in such an illogical manner? We can point to a parallel situation here on our own planet. Why, given our own relatively advanced technology and level of knowledge, is bureaucratic infighting delaying the construction of the space stations? Why is NASA nearly bankrupt?

We also can look at examples in areas other than space science. Why would politicians lobby for tighter controls on cigarettes because of cancer dangers, but pass bills that would subsidize farmers to grow tobacco? Why do bureaucrats create subcommittees to investigate wastes of time and taxpayers' money? Why would politicians sponsor a covert activity to break into a psychiatrist's office in a hotel? (For that matter, why would people vote for politicians, knowing their track records for honesty and integrity?) Why can't my subscription to a magazine get renewed, even when I send the check in four months before the subscription expires? And why are 60 percent of all automobiles recalled by the manufacturer during the first year they are on the road?

The answer, of course, is incompetence. Bureaucratic bungling, political wrangling, and general ineptitude are responsible for most of the problems in the world today. Politicians and bureaucrats create such confusion that it is clear they themselves have no idea what they are doing.

Now, imagine a highly evolved technical civilization on a distant planet. Its society functions well, with the exception of a comparatively small number of its population. These would no doubt be their most ineffective politicians and bureaucrats. What better way to remove them from the general gene pool and workforce than to send them off on interstellar voyages that, with relativity, would return them many, many years later, if at all?

Because they are incompetent, they would be confused as to their mission. They would be clumsy pilots and navigators and, because they lack the true knowledge of their society, they would be unable to tell anyone anything about their purpose or scientific capability with any degree of understanding or common sense.

As evidence that this is true, a cursory study of the terrestrial government cover-up of UFO crashes shows incompetence as well, but this time with regard to human bureaucrats. The presence of a vast number of leaked documents shows that the government (even a "shadow" variety) cannot function effectively because it is, after all, still a government (which, by definition, is incompetent).

Therefore, we can observe that bizarre aspects of the UFO phenomenon are explained best by assuming the aliens are incompetent. More to the point, they must be the most incompetent examples of their race, namely the bureaucrats. The Alien Incompetency Theory is borne out by an examination of the available observations and claims of witnesses, and can finally explain what is going on. An understanding of this situation will certainly change the way ufologists will approach their subject.

March 1996
Winnipeg, Canada

Thirteen
MAGICAL THINKING

OF ALL THE SIGNS OF millennialism, evidence of magical thinking is perhaps the most prevalent in the last few years before the turn of the century, having far outstripped apocalypticism, doomsayers, and even alienmongers as a sign of the emerging New Age. Magical thinking can be defined as the imbuing of ordinary objects with extraordinary powers or properties. Hence we have such things as the rise of crystal therapy, herbalism, aromatherapy, and healing movements of all kinds. Meditation, imaging, and creative visualization can also be gathered under the magical-thinking umbrella, as such practices make the claim that thinking itself changes reality.

Magical thinking is significant to millennialists because it represents an important synthesis of ancient traditions with contemporary movements toward healing, wholeness, and empowerment. Magical thinking, though it may be considered unendurably naive by some, is optimism at its most basic. Derived largely from "lost" cultures and belief systems, magical thinking returns a sense of power to the individual. And as we make our way toward the millennium, the rise in the use of such systems of belief by ordinary people is a very hopeful sign indeed.

Whether or not you happen to believe, for example, that the essence of ambergris (which by the way is a form of whale vomit), will raise your personal level of spiritual vibration is unimportant. What matters is that ideas like spiritual vibration exist at all—that they have fired the public imagination. Further, the need to "raise" those vibrations to a level of greater attunement with invisible energies, cosmic forces, or what have you is a collective sign of hope and renewal. It means that large numbers of people have grown weary of the doomsayers, tired of the apocalyptics, and are ready to believe in something once again. That magical thinking brings the need to believe down to relatively mundane levels is also unimportant when one considered the simplicity, the sense of harmony, and the range of experience evoked by such systems.

The recent resurrection of Native American religions, shamanic traditions, and the like can be seen as more than the naive yearnings for new religious allegories or the conscience-stricken backtracking of anxiety-ridden imperialists. Instead, such revivals of old belief systems can, on the threshold of a millennium, represent the making of individual and collective peace with the natural environment—a way of relinquishing contemporary fears of overpopulation, pollution, and planetary catastrophe. If we better understand the earth through such practices, we better appreciate the fact that nature is not "out to get us." Our sense of who we are and where we belong in the greater scheme of things is restored.

Through magical thinking, the relationship between man and his enivronment is reestablished and reintegrated. As a result, mankind becomes less alienated, less frightened, and less convinced of some impending catastrophe.

By and large, magical thinking is psychologically very useful in that such movements are generally associated with ideas such as "wholeness," "wellness," and "longevity." They serve to strengthen collective belief in the future through continuity of knowledge and traditions. They empower individuals by moving to synthesize the world of the "lower" self with that of a "higher" self. The past is reconciled with the present, the old with the new, and anxiety with hope.

Further, magical thinking is just plain harmless. Nobody ever died from an overdose of chamomile tea and nobody ever went irrevocably mad from burning too much incense or sniffing essence of begonia. Nobody ever started a war meditating under a pyramid or carrying a particular crystal in their pocket. In fact, many magical belief systems cause us to focus our energy in highly positive ways. If employees of the World Bank take a meditation break each day to, as has been reported, "send out waves of positive energy," they are hurting no one and nothing by doing so. And, in fact, if we humans can shape our future simply by the way we think about the future, they may be doing some good, if only because they believe that they are.

Magical beliefs also reassure us that everything we need to survive is readily available in the natural world—all we have to do to ensure survival is to protect that world. Most such systems rely on "natural" cures, "organic" foods, herbs, essences, and materials such as crystals or geometric shapes. They represent a highly democratic approach to personal empowerment, using relatively ordinary, readily available materials. In short, one does not have to be a magician to be a magical thinker, but magical thinking can empower people to the extent that they feel like magicians, because through such practices ordinary reality is transformed—imbued with extraordinary properties.

Moreover, the tradition of magical belief systems represent a rich storehouse of cultural knowledge. They open our eyes to beauty, they open our ears to the stories and wisdom of the ages, and they protect and synthesize against the loss of identity through the continuity of human tradition. Magical thinking is also important because its traditional precepts hold that the human mind and spirit have vast untapped resources, nearly unlimited potential. As such, they endow us with a new frontier—a frontier of self. The future becomes exciting once again, because there are things yet to be discovered, miracles yet to be performed.

Thus, the "magic" of magical thinking is our own magic, home-brewed and utterly non-threatening, non-invasive and rather comforting all around.

Magical thinking gives us a very real alternative to ordinary thinking, and sometimes very real insight into the nature of existence. It transforms us into magicians by focusing our attention away from anxiety and restoring our sense of control over our lives. We are taught that each of us has natural "powers," and through magical thinking we can align and join our powers with other invisible forces. By doing so, we can successfully remove the threat of the unknown inherent in those invisible forces and get on with the business of living. Through such "magical" thinking the god within becomes successfully joined to the god without.

If we have lived with paranoia for too long, the rise in magical thinking tells us that we're ready to give up our fears in the interest of renewal and transformation. In that, the so-called "natural" or "alternative systems" of "healing" so widely in use today can be interpreted quite literally. They are both natural and do constitute a viable alternative to rampant paranoia. By changing our thinking, we can be healed—or at the very least, considerably reassured.

Finally, the dramatic rise in the use of magical belief systems here on the threshold of the New Age is so significant because through their resurrection newer and more radical examples of synthesis between old and new knowledge are taking place all the time. It was recently reported that the Pentagon appropriated millions of dollars in funding to study the healing method of "laying on of hands" under laboratory conditions. With any number of movements afoot to study non-scientific practices under scientific conditions, who knows what we may discover about our powers over reality? It might just be that we stand at the edge of a very New Age indeed.

AFTERWARD . . .

THE CHANCE TO STEP back from the material itself and pontificate at the end of a book like this one is nearly irresistible. However, there is more than enough intense rhetoric surrounding the turn of the coming century. I will let the scholars debate over the endless nuances of millennialism and the cutural revolution; I'll let the clerics discuss the signs of the apocalypse, and the paranoids whisper their theories of conspiracy and chaos, and keep my own comments as mercifully short as possible.

Even at its direst, the millennium legend always makes for the provision of hope. If the world is to be destroyed, it's worth a reminder that no one has ever believed or predicted that we will be entirely destroyed. If the prophets and mystics have cautioned us throughout the course of history to clean up our collective act as a means of avoiding or preparing for a Great Transformation, cleaning up our act is not bad advice at any point in history. Being human, there is always room for improvement. We can always be a little kinder, a little less aggressive, a little more concerned with the collective good.

Much of what millennialism constitutes is an opportunity to pause and take stock of ourselves and our world. This fascinating period leading up to the turn of the year 2000 is not our final exam so much as is an intense review session. Yes, it can give rise to a host of fears about what may come, but, as a species, we humans do very well with fear. It has served us for centuries on end as our principle adaptive coping mechanism. Fear has always helped us ensure survival. Whatever else the millennium may hold, it appears at least that we mean to survive.

And for human beings, the business of survival is not a business based on faint hopes and empty imaginings. Survival is no mere pipe dream here on planet earth, it is an imperative. But with so many of our basic survival needs attended to, we have been afforded the luxury of allowing ourselves not a little bit of grand speculation about this millennial feeling and have come up (courtesy of the cerebral cortex— that great creative god within) with any number of truly fascinating explanations for why we feel the way that we feel. A consensus of opinion on the reasons and explanations for our feelings, while it cannot always be said to constitute physical reality, can certainly be said to constitute our cultural and (for want of a better term) "spiritual" reality. In reviewing ourselves, we have at our disposal a vast wealth of symbols, allegories, and cultural traditions to draw upon as we seek meaning and identity in the universe.

It is part of our nature to tell ourselves stories about life and what it means to be human. It is arguably the best part of our nature, for it is this impulse that gives rise to art, to religion, to civilization as we know it. It is this part of our nature that transcends the notion of life as mere survival. But the reality of the collective is not a static reality, any more than physical reality is static. It is always changing, always discovering, if not new meanings in life, then new ways to describe meaning. A fiery chariot becomes a spaceship, a winged god an angel, then an alien as we attempt to sort our way through our symbolic language, discarding those symbols and descriptions which are no longer meaningful and finding new names and symbols for that which is. This does not so much point to a decline of civilization as it points to an evolution of it. Whether that evolution must be preceded by some widespread planetary destruction or purification is a matter of opinion. Certainly many of our cultural traditions and symbols would indicate as much.

But, for all of that, symbols are not reality, they are descriptions of feelings about reality. And like any language, symbolic language is sometimes inept, oftentimes inadequate, and too frequently words are taken literally at the expense of meaning. Yet on the threshold of the millennium, our angels are still with us, our demons, too, as our fears and our hopes continue struggling to win the battle for meaning in the coming century.

But all the signs would indicate that hope has already won, if only because we mean to survive. We are living in the midst of the New Age, not merely waiting for it. The New Age, for all of its merchandising, lunacy, and apparent silliness, is a movement that reempowers individuals and restores their sense of control over their own lives. Through the contemporary revival of all manner of systems of "magical thinking" and "therapies" of all kinds, we are reintegrating ancient tradition in modern life. We are making the necessary peace with the planet and with ourselves. Through magical thinking, we are becoming more magical, restoring and renewing and transforming ourselves. We are "healing" the rift between physical reality and spiritual reality, becoming both individually and collectively more "whole" than was possible when our fears for survival so divided us. The New Age of our dreams did not begin on any specific date, any more than the Renaissance did. It is a hard truth that transformation happens only by degrees, however we might wish it otherwise. But we are making progress, if only by those same degrees. The worst of our fears for the future have given way to the need to redefine and reshape the present.

And that alone is cause for a great celebration.

Why wait for New Year's Eve?